TABLE OF CONTENTS

BREAKFAST

COCONUT BUTTER OATMEAL

Preparation time: 5 minutes

Cooking time: 4 hours and 30 minutes

Serving: 2

Ingredients:

- ½ cup coconut flakes
- 1 ½ cups coconut milk
- 1 teaspoon vanilla extract
- 2 tablespoons coconut sugar
- 4 tablespoons coconut butter

Directions:

- In your slow cooker, combine all the ingredients, stir, cover and cook on high for 4 hours and 30 minutes.
- Stir the oatmeal one more time and serve for breakfast while warm.

Nutrition:

- Calories - 522
- Fat - 49,6
- Carbs - 35,7

- Protein - 8,8

CASSEROLE BREAKFAST

Serving: 2

Ingredients:

- 2 large eggs
- Pinch of salt
- Pinch of black pepper
- ¼ teaspoon thyme
- ¼ teaspoon garlic powder
- ¼ teaspoon onion powder
- 2 tablespoons milk
- ¼ cup Greek yogurt
- ¼ cup mushrooms, diced
- ½ cup ham, diced
- ½ cup baby spinach
- ½ cup Monterey Jack cheese, shredded
- Non-stick cooking spray

Directions:

- In a medium mixing bowl, crack the eggs and add the salt, pepper, thyme, garlic powder, onion powder, milk, and yogurt.
- Whisk all the ingredients together.
- Stir the mushrooms, ham, cheese, and spinach into the bowl.
- Spray the slow cooker with non-stick spray and pour the egg mixture into it.
- Cover, and set the temperature to HIGH. Cook for 1 ½ to 2 hours.
- Remove the casserole carefully from the cooker and slice it before serving.

Nutrition:

- Calories - 243
- Fat - 13 g
- Carbs - 10 g
- Protein - 52 g

LEEK AND TURKEY BREAKFAST MIX

Preparation time: 5 minutes

Cooking time: 7 hours

Serving: 4

Ingredients:

- 2 cups leeks, chopped
- 2 tablespoons olive oil

- 1 cup mustard greens, torn
- 2 garlic cloves, minced
- 8 eggs, whisked
- 1 ½ cups turkey fillet, cooked and chopped

Directions:

- Heat up a pan with the oil over medium heat, add the turkey, stir, and let it brown for 5 minutes then Add the rest of the ingredients to the slow cooker as well, toss them to combine well, cover and cook on low for 7 hours.
- Divide everything between plates and serve for breakfast.

Nutrition:

- Calories - 281
- Fat - 16,2
- Carbs - 8,2
- Protein - 26

ITALIAN OMELET WITH HERBS

Preparation + Cooking time: 20 minutes

Serving: 2

Ingredients:

- For omelet: ½ medium-sized tomato, chopped
- 3 large eggs
- 2 garlic cloves, crushed
- Spices: 2 tbsp olive oil
- ½ tsp sea salt
- 1 tsp Italian seasoning mix

Directions:

- Grease the inner pot with two tablespoons of olive oil and press the "Saute" button. Heat up and add tomatoes. Cook for 2-3 minutes, stirring constantly.
- Now add garlic and season with Italian seasoning mix. Continue to cook for another 1-2 minute. Remove from the pot and Meanwhile, in a small bowl, whisk the eggs together. Pour the mixture in the pot and continue to cook for 2-3 minutes or until set.
- Press the "Cancel" button and gently remove the inner pot. Using a wooden spatula, loosen the edges and remove the eggs.
- Add tomatoes and fold over.
- Serve immediately.

Nutrition:

- Calories - 235
- Fat - 21.5g
- Carbs - 1.9g

- Protein - 9.8g

BACON BRUSSELS SPROUTS

Preparation + Cooking time: 15 minutes

Serving: 3

Ingredients:

- 1 cup Brussels sprouts, chopped
- 3 oz bacon, cut into bite-sized pieces
- 4 large eggs, beaten
- 1 tbsp green onions, finely chopped
- 1 tbsp olive oil
- 1 tbsp balsamic vinegar
- Spices: 1 tsp garlic powder
- ½ tsp smoked paprika, ground
- 1 tsp sea salt

Directions:

- Plug in your instant pot and grease the stainless steel insert with olive oil. Press the "Saute" button and add Brussels sprouts. Sprinkle with garlic powder, paprika and salt.
- Stir well and cook for 5 minutes.
- Now, add beaten eggs, onions, and balsamic vinegar. Give it a good stir and cook for 2-3 more minutes. Turn off the pot and stir in the bacon immediately.
- Let it stand for 10 minutes before serving.

Nutrition:

- Calories - 307
- Fat - 23.3g
- Carbs - 3.3g
- Protein - 20.1g

BREAKFAST MEATLOAF

Preparation time: 18 minutes

Cooking time: 7 hours

Serving: 8

Ingredients:

- 12 oz. ground beef
- 1 teaspoon salt
- 1 teaspoon ground coriander
- 1 tablespoon ground mustard
- ¼ teaspoon ground chili pepper

- 6 oz. white bread
- ½ cup milk
- 1 teaspoon ground black pepper
- 3 tablespoon tomato sauce

Directions:

- Chop the white bread and combine it with the milk.
- Stir then set aside for 3 minutes.
- Meanwhile, combine the ground beef, salt, ground coriander, ground mustard, ground chili pepper, and ground black pepper.
- Stir the white bread mixture carefully and add it to the ground beef. Cover the bottom of the slow cooker bowl with foil.
- Shape the meatloaf and place the uncooked meatloaf in the slow cooker then spread it with the tomato sauce.
- Close the slow cooker lid and cook the meatloaf for 7 hours on LOW.
- Slice the prepared meatloaf and serve. Enjoy!

Nutrition:

- Calories - 214
- Fat - 14
- Carbs - 12.09
- Protein - 9

QUAIL OMELET

Preparation time: 10 minutes

Cooking time: 1.5 hours

Serving: 2

Ingredients:

- 6 quail eggs
- ½ teaspoon salt
- ¾ teaspoon ground black pepper
- 3 tablespoons cream cheese
- ½ teaspoon butter, melted

Directions:

- Beat the quail eggs in the bowl and whisk them with the help of the hand whisker.
- Add salt, ground black pepper, and cream cheese. Mix up the mixture.
- But melted butter in the crockpot.
- Add egg liquid and close the lid.
- Cook the omelet for 1.5 hours on High.

Nutrition:

- Calories - 105
- Fat - 9.2
- Carbs - 1
- Protein - 4.8

INDIAN GREENS BREAKFAST

Preparation time: 10 minutes

Cooking time: 4 hours

Serving: 4

Ingredients:

- 1 pound mustard leaves
- 2 tablespoons vegetable stock
- 2 tablespoons olive oil
- 1 teaspoon ginger, grated
- 2 red onions, chopped
- 4 garlic cloves, minced
- 1 teaspoon ground cu minutes
- 1 teaspoon garam masala
- ½ teaspoon turmeric powder
- A pinch of salt and black pepper

Directions:

- In your slow cooker, combine all the ingredients, mix, cover and cook on high for 4 hours.
- Divide the mixture into bowls and serve it for breakfast.

Nutrition:

- Calories - 107
- Fat - 7,5
- Carbs - 9,2
- Protein - 3,3

QUINOA CURRY

Preparation time: 20 minutes

Cooking time: 9 hours

Serving: 7

Ingredients:

- 8 oz. potato
- 7 oz. cauliflower

- 1 cup onion, chopped
- 7 oz. chickpea, canned
- 1 cup tomatoes, chopped
- 13 oz. almond milk
- 3 cup chicken stock
- 8 tablespoon quinoa
- 1/3 tablespoon miso
- 1 teaspoon minced garlic
- 2 teaspoon curry paste

Directions:

- Peel the potatoes and chop them.
- Put the chopped potatoes, onion, and tomatoes into the slow cooker. Combine the miso, chicken stock, and curry paste together.
- Whisk the mixture until the ingredients are dissolved in the chicken stock. Pour the chicken stock in the slow cooker too.
- Separate the cauliflower into the florets.
- Add the cauliflower florets and the chickpeas in the slow cooker.
- Add the almond milk, quinoa, and minced garlic.
- Close the slow cooker lid and cook the dish on the LOW for 9 hours.
- When the dish is cooked, chill it and then mix it gently.

Nutrition:

- Calories - 262
- Fat - 4.6
- Carbs - 44.31
- Protein - 12

TOTER TOTS CASSEROLE

Preparation time: 10 minutes

Cooking time: 3 hours

Serving: 8

Ingredients:

- 8 oz tater tots
- 1 cup ground beef
- 3 oz Cheddar cheese, shredded
- 1 tablespoon butter
- ¼ cup heavy cream
- ½ teaspoon salt

Directions:

- Mix up together ground beef and salt.
- Place butter in the crockpot and make the layer of ground beef.

- Then arrange tater tots over the beef.
- Top the casserole with Cheddar cheese and heavy cream.
- Close the lid and cook the casserole for 3 hours on High.

Nutrition:

- Calories - 155
- Fat - 10.8
- Carbs - 8.1
- Protein - 6.6

CHEDDAR BACON POTATO

Preparation time: 8-10 minutes

Cooking time: 7 minutes

Serving: 2

Ingredients:

- 1/2 teaspoon garlic powder
- 1 1/2 ounces cheddar cheese, grated
- 1 ounces ranch dressing
- 1 teaspoon parsley, dried
- 1/2 pound red potatoes, make medium size cubes
- 1 bacon strip, chopped
- A pinch of pepper and salt
- 1 tablespoon water

Directions:

- Take your 3-Quart Instant Pot; open the top lid. Plug it and turn it on.
- In the cooking pot area, add the bacon, parsley, salt, potatoes, pepper, garlic powder, and water.
- Using a spatula, stir the ingredients.
- Close the top lid and seal its valve.
- Press "MANUAL" setting. Adjust cooking time to 7 minutes.
- Allow the recipe to cook for the set cooking time.
- After the set cooking time ends, press "CANCEL" and then press "QPR (Quick Pressure Release".
- Instant Pot will quickly release the pressure.
- Open the top lid, add the cooked recipe mix in serving plates. Mix in the cheese and dressing.

Nutrition:

- Calories - 296
- Fat - 9.5g
- Carbs - 41g
- Protein - 13g

FETA EGG BITES

Preparation time: 10 minutes

Cooking time: 2 hours

Serving: 2

Ingredients:

- 3 egg, beaten
- 1 tablespoon almond flour
- 2 oz Feta, crumbled
- 1/3 teaspoon salt
- 1 teaspoon butter, melted
- ½ cup water, for cooking

Directions:

- Mix up together eggs, almond flour, crumbled Feta, salt, and melted butter.
- Pour the homogenous liquid into the non-sticky muffin molds.
- Pour water in the crockpot.
- Arrange the muffin molds in the crockpot and close the lid.
- Cook egg bites for 2 hours on high.

Nutrition:

- Calories - 266
- Fat - 21.5
- Carbs - 4.7
- Protein - 15.4

PEPPERS, YAMS AND TURKEY DELIGHT

Preparation time: 5 minutes

Cooking time: 6 hours

Serving: 4

Ingredients:

- 3 yams, peeled and cubed
- 1 green bell pepper, cubed
- 1 red bell pepper, cubed
- 1 orange bell pepper, cubed
- 1 red onion, chopped
- 12 ounces smoked turkey, sliced
- 1 cup cream of coconut
- ½ teaspoon oregano, dried
- 2 tablespoons cilantro, chopped

Directions:

- Combine all the ingredients in your slow cooker, reserving the cilantro.
- Mix well, cover and cook on low for 6 hours.
- Divide between four plates, sprinkle the cilantro on top and serve.

Nutrition:

- Calories - 597
- Fat - 43,8
- Carbs - 34,9
- Protein - 19,6

ASPARAGUS WITH COTTAGE CHEESE

Preparation + Cooking time: 25 minutes

Serving: 2

Ingredients:

- 1 cup asparagus, trimmed and chopped
- ½ cup cottage cheese, crumbled
- 2 tbsp Greek yogurt, full-cream
- 4 large eggs, beaten
- 2 garlic cloves, finely chopped
- 1 tbsp olive oil
- Spices: 1 tsp salt
- ¼ tsp chili pepper, ground
- 2 tsp balsamic vinegar
- ¼ tsp black pepper, ground

Directions:

- Rinse the asparagus under cold running water and trim off the woody ends.
- Cut into bite-sized pieces and set aside.
- Plug in your instant pot and pour one cup of water in the stainless steel insert. Position a trivet on the bottom and place a steam basket on top. Add the asparagus and sprinkle with some salt. Close the lid and adjust the steam release handle.
- Press the "Steam" button and set the timer for 10 minutes.
- When done, perform a quick release of the pressure and open the pot. Remove the steam basket and water from the pot and wipe with a kitchen paper.
- Now, add olive oil to the stainless steel insert and press the "Saute" button. Add garlic and cook for 1 minute. Add eggs, cheese, and yogurt. Sprinkle with chili, salt, and pepper. Cook for 3-4 minutes, or until eggs are set.
- Turn off the pot.
- Serve immediately.

Nutrition:

- Calories - 289

- Fat - 18.6g
- Carbs - 5.9g
- Protein - 24.1g

APPLE BREAKFAST FRITTATA PIE

Preparation time: 15 minutes

Cooking time: 3 hours

Serving: 8

Ingredients:

- 7 oz. mozzarella, sliced
- 10 eggs
- 1 cup milk
- 3 tablespoon flour
- 1 teaspoon salt
- 1 teaspoon chili flakes
- ½ cup cherry tomatoes, chopped
- 1 red sweet pepper
- 1 yellow sweet pepper
- 1 apple
- 1 teaspoon butter

Directions:

- Crack the eggs into the bowl and mix them up with the help of the hand mixer.
- After this, pour the milk into the mixture. Add the flour, salt, chili flakes, and butter.
- Then peel the apple and chop it. Add the chopped apple to the egg mixture.
- Remove the seeds from the sweet peppers and chop them into the small pieces.
- Whisk the egg mixture with the flour until it has dissolved and then add the chopped vegetables. Then pour the egg mixture into the slow cooker and make a layer of the sliced mozzarella on top.
- Close the slow cooker lid and cook frittata pie for 3 hours on LOW. Cut the prepared dish into the slices. Enjoy!

Nutrition:

- Calories - 252
- Fat - 13.7
- Carbs - 11.25
- Protein - 21

BROCCOLI EGG MORNING

Preparation time: 5-8 minutes

Cooking time: 5 minutes

Serving: 2

Ingredients:

- 3 eggs, whisked
- ½ cup broccoli florets
- A pinch garlic powder
- 2 tablespoons tomatoes
- 1 clove garlic, minced
- ½ small yellow onion, chopped
- ½ red bell pepper, chopped
- 2 tablespoons cheese, grated
- A pinch chili powder
- 2 tablespoons onions
- 2 tablespoons parsley
- Pepper and salt as needed

Directions:

- Take your 3-Quart Instant Pot; open the top lid. Plug it and turn it on.
- Open the top lid; grease inside cooking surface using a cooking spray.
- In a bowl, whisk the eggs.
- Add the remaining ingredients except the cheese. Season with Pepper and salt.
- In the cooking pot area, add the mixture.
- Close the top lid and seal its valve.
- Press "STEAM" setting. Adjust cooking time to 5 minutes.
- Allow the recipe to cook for the set cooking time.
- After the set cooking time ends, press "CANCEL" and then press "QPR (Quick Pressure Release)".
- Instant Pot will quickly release the pressure.
- Open the top lid, add the cooked recipe mix in serving plates.
- Top with the cheese.
- Serve and enjoy!

Nutrition:

- Calories - 376
- Fat - 28g
- Carbs - 9g
- Protein - 23g

SAUSAGE EGG QUICHE

Ingredients:

- 2 teaspoons vanilla extract
- 1/8 teaspoon nutmeg, ground
- 1 small zucchini, peeled, grated
- ½ cup pecans, chopped
- 1/8 teaspoon cloves, ground
- 3/4 teaspoon cinnamon

- 1 large peeled carrot, grated
- 1 cup steel cut oats
- 3 cups almond milk or soy milk (vanilla flavored
- 4 tablespoons maple syrup

Directions:

- Take your Instant Pot and place it on a clean kitchen platform. Turn it on after plugging it into a power socket.
- Open the lid from the top and put it aside; start adding the mentioned ingredients inside and gently stir them.
- Close the lid and lock. Ensure that you have sealed the valve to avoid leakage.
- Press "Slow Cook" mode and set the timer to 3 hours. It will take a few minutes for the pot to build inside pressure and start cooking.
- After the timer reads zero, press "Cancel" and quick release pressure.
- Carefully remove the lid and serve warm!

Nutrition:

- Calories - 384
- Fat - 19g
- Carbs - 22.5g
- Protein - 5g

SAUSAGE AND EGG CASSEROLE

Serving: 6-8

Ingredients:

- 8 eggs, beaten
- 1 sweet potato, peeled and grated
- 1 pound pork country-style sausage, chopped or ground pork sausage meat
- 2 tablespoons coconut oil (optional plus a little extra for greasing
- 1 medium onion, minced
- ½ cup green onion, chopped
- 1 ½ teaspoons garlic powder
- 2 teaspoons dried basil
- sea salt and black pepper, to taste

Directions:

- Line the inside of the slow cooker with parchment paper and grease with oil (This can be used as a handle later, to easily pull out the finished product).
- Heat the oil in a skillet over a medium heat and saute the chopped sausage until
- slightly browned at edges (about 3-5 minutes). Remove from heat.
- Add all the ingredients to the slow cooker.
- Cook on LOW for 6 hours or until set.

Nutrition:

- Calories - 196
- Fat - 10.4 g
- Carbs - 6 g
- Protein - 18.6 g

CREAMY MILLET

Preparation time: 8 minutes

Cooking time: 4 hours 10 minutes

Serving: 6

Ingredients:

- 3 cup millet
- 6 cup chicken stock
- 1 teaspoon salt
- 4 tablespoon heavy cream
- 5 oz. bacon, chopped

Directions:

- Put the millet and chicken stock in the slow cooker bowl and mix.
- Add salt and chopped bacon.
- Close the slow cooker lid and cook the dish on HIGH for 4 hours or until the millet absorbs all the liquid.
- Then add the heavy cream and mix.
- Cook the dish on HIGH for 10 minutes more.
- Mix carefully one more time and

Nutrition:

- Calories - 572
- Fat - 17.8
- Carbs - 83.09
- Protein - 20

EGG MUFFINS

Preparation time: 10 minutes

Cooking time: 2 hours

Serving: 4

Ingredients:

- 4 eggs, beaten
- 4 teaspoons heavy cream
- 4 teaspoons almond flour

- 1/3 teaspoon ground black pepper
- 1 oz Parmesan, grated
- 1 oz bacon, chopped, cooked
- Cooking spray
- ½ cup water, for cooking

Directions:

- Whisk together eggs, heavy cream, almond flour, and ground black pepper.
- Then add grated Parmesan and chopped bacon. Stir it gently.
- Spray the muffin molds with cooking spray and pour egg mixture inside them.
- Pour the water in the crockpot and arrange the muffin molds.
- Close the crockpot lid and cook muffins for 2 hours on High.
- Chill the cooked egg muffins well and then remove them from the molds.

Nutrition:

- Calories - 302
- Fat - 24.7
- Carbs - 7
- Protein - 16.6

VEGETABLES AND VEGETERIAN

RAJMA MASALA WITH CAULIFLOWER

Preparation + Cooking time: 25 minutes

Serving: 4

Ingredients:

- 1 lb cauliflower, cut into florets
- 1 cup cherry tomatoes, chopped
- 1 small onion, finely chopped
- 3 chili peppers, chopped
- 4 tbsp ghee
- 3 tbsp oil
- 3 cups vegetable stock

Spices:

- 2 tbsp coriander seeds
- 1 tsp salt
- 2 tbsp chili powder
- 3 tsp garam masala
- 1 tbsp fresh ginger, grated
- ¼ cup fresh parsley, finely chopped

Directions:

- Grease the inner pot with oil and add coriander seeds and chili peppers.
- Cook for 3-4 minutes, stirring constantly.
- Now add onions and season with all spices. Stir well and continue to cook for another 3-4 minutes.
- Add the remaining ingredients and pour in the stock. Stir well and seal the lid. Set the steam release handle to the "Sealing" position and press the "MANUAL" button.
- Set the timer for 15 minutes on high pressure.
- When done, release the pressure naturally and open the lid.
- Serve immediately.

Nutrition:

- Calories - 251
- Fat - 23.3g
- Carbs - 6g
- Protein - 3.2g

CREAMY BEAN AND ARTICHOKE DIP

Serving: 8

Cooking time: 15 minutes

Preparation time: 50 minutes

Ingredients:

- ½ cup dry cannellini beans, soaked overnight
- 8 medium-sized artichokes, cleaned and trimmed
- 1 cup water
- ½ lemon, juiced
- 2 cloves of garlic, minced
- ¾ cup plain non-fat yogurt
- 1 teaspoon salt
- ¼ teaspoon pepper
- ¾ cup grated Parmigiano cheese

Directions:

- Place the beans, artichokes, and water in the Instant Pot.
- Close the lid and press the Bean/Chili button.
- Adjust the cooking time to 50 minutes.
- Do quick pressure release.
- Drain the beans and allow to remove excess water.
- In a food processor, place the beans and artichokes.
- Season with lemon juice, garlic, yogurt, salt, and pepper.
- Pulse until smooth.
- Add the grated Parmigiano cheese.

Nutrition:

- Calories - 134
- Carbs - 20.95g
- Protein - 9.36g
- Fat - 3.27g

COCONUT CABBAGE IN CROCK POT

Serving: 6

Ingredients:

- 2 tablespoons coconut oil
- 2 red onions, peeled and sliced
- Salt, to taste
- 2 teaspoons garlic, diced
- 1 teaspoon red chili, sliced
- 1 tablespoon mustard seeds
- 2 tablespoons curry powder
- ½ tablespoon turmeric powder
- 3 cups cabbage, shredded
- 2 cups carrot, peeled and sliced
- ¼ cup lemon juice
- 1 cup coconut milk, unsweetened

Directions:

- Press the BROWN/SAUTe button of the Crock-Pot Express and turn it on.
- Preheat the pot and then add the oil, onion, garlic.
- Cook until aromatic.
- Add salt, red chili, mustard seed, curry powder, turmeric powder, lemon juice and let cook for a few seconds.
- Add the carrots and cabbage and pour in the water.
- Press the START/STOP button and then press the STEAM button.
- Set the timer for 5 minutes at high pressure.
- After 5 minutes, release the steam.
- Open the pot and then add coconut milk.
- Stir it a few times and then serve.

Nutrition:

- Calories - 191
- Fat - 15.1 g
- Carbs - 14.1 g
- Protein - 3 g

VEGETARIAN GUMBO

Serving: 6

Ingredients:

- 2 cups frozen, cut okra, thawed
- 2 teaspoons Cajun seasoning
- 2 15-ounce cans black beans, rinsed and drained
- 1 16-ounce package frozen diced sweet peppers and onions
- 1 28-ounce can
- diced
- fire-roasted tomatoes, undrained

Directions:

- Combine all the ingredients in the slow cooker.
- Cover and cook for 6-8 hours on LOW.
- Serve.

Nutrition:

- Calories - 153
- Fat - 0.8 g
- Carbs - 31 g
- Protein - 12 g

SUN-DRIED TOMATO POLENTA

Serving: 8

Cooking time: 2 minutes

Preparation time: 10 minutes

Ingredients:

- 2 tablespoons olive oil
- 2 cloves of garlic, minced
- ½ cup onion, chopped
- 4 cups vegetable stock
- 1/3 cup sun-dried tomatoes, finely chopped
- 1 bay leaf
- 1 teaspoon salt
- 2 tablespoons parsley, chopped
- 2 teaspoons oregano, chopped
- 3 tablespoons basil, chopped
- 1 teaspoon rosemary, chopped
- 1 cup polenta

Directions:

- Press the Saute button on the Instant Pot and add the oil.
- Saute the garlic and onions for 3 minutes until fragrant.
- Add the stock, sun-dried tomatoes, bay leaf, salt, parsley, oregano, basil, and rosemary. Stir to combine.
- Sprinkle polenta on top but do not stir.

- Close the lid and adjust the cooking time to 5 minutes.
- Do natural pressure release.

Nutrition:

- Calories - 69
- Carbs - 8.48g
- Protein - 1.07g
- Fat - 3.61g

CAULIFLOWER SPREAD WITH THYME

Preparation + Cooking time: 25 minutes

Serving: 6

Ingredients:

- 1 lb cauliflower, chopped into florets
- 2 chili peppers, diced
- ½ cup canned tomatoes, sugar-free
- 3 tbsp butter
- ¼ cup heavy cream
- ¼ cup cream cheese
- 2 tbsp Parmesan cheese
- 2 tbsp apple cider vinegar
- Spices: 1 tsp salt
- ½ red pepper flakes
- ½ tsp white pepper
- 2 tsp dried thyme

Directions:

- Plug in the instant pot and grease the inner pot with butter. Press the "Saute" button and add peppers. Briefly cook, for 2 mintues and then add canned tomatoes. Season with salt and one teaspoon of thyme.
- Continue to cook for 4-5 minuts, stirring occasionally.
- Now add cauliflower and season with the remaining thyme, pepper flakes, and white pepper. Pour in one cup of water and seal the lid.
- Set the steam release handle to the "Sealing" position and press the "MANUAL" button.
- Cook for 12 minutes on high pressure.
- When done, perform a quick pressure release and open the lid. Chill for a while and Process until smooth.

Nutrition:

- Calories - 140
- Fat - 12.1g
- Carbs - 3.1g
- Protein - 4g

ZUCCHINI EGGPLANT WITH CUCUMBER SAUCE

Preparation + Cooking time: 20 minutes

Serving: 3

Ingredients:

- 1-eggplant; sliced
- 2 garlic cloves; finely chopped
- 1 small chili pepper; finely chopped
- 1 small zucchini; sliced
- 1 tablespoon olive oil
- For the sauce: 1/2 teaspoon onion powder
- 1 cucumber; sliced
- 1/4 teaspoon black pepper; ground
- 1/4 teaspoon cayenne pepper; ground
- 1/2 cup sour cream
- 1 tablespoon fresh chives; finely chopped
- 1/2 teaspoon salt

Directions:

- Combine all sauce ingredients in a food processor and blend until smooth and creamy, Set aside
- Plug in the instant pot and press the "SAUTE" button. Heat up the olive oil and add garlic and chili pepper. Cook for 2-3 minutes, stirring constantly.
- Add eggplant and zucchini. Sprinkle with some salt and cook for 2 minutes on each side
- Pour in the vegetable broth and close the lid. Set the steam release handle and press the "MANUAL" button. Set the timer for 4 minutes and cook on "HIGH" pressure.
- When done, perform a quick pressure release and open the pot a serving plate and drizzle with cucumber sauce. Optionally, sprinkle with some lemon juice and enjoy!

Nutrition:

- Calories - 188
- Fat - 13.2g
- Carbs - 10.3g
- Protein - 4.1g

PAPRIKA POTATO APPETIZER

Preparation time: 8-10 minutes

Cooking time: 20 minutes

Serving: 2

Ingredients:

- 1 tablespoon dry mango powder

- 2 tablespoons vegetable oil
- 1 teaspoon paprika
- 3 large sweet potatoes, peeled and make wedges
- ½ teaspoon salt
- 1 cup water
- Cooking oil as needed.
- Set Instant Pot to Saute and add oil, followed by ham or salt pork. Brown, then add onion and garlic. Cook until onion is Add molasses, maple syrup, mustard powder, Worcestershire sauce, ketchup, salt, and pepper to the pot. Add beans and stir to combine. Pour in water.
- Close lid and set cooking time for 30 minutes at high pressure.
- When beans are cooked, season to taste with salt, pepper, Worcestershire, and sugar.

Directions:

- Switch on the pot after placing it on a clean and dry platform.
- Pour 1 cup water into the pot. Arrange the trivet inside it; arrange the wedges over the trivet.
- Close the pot by closing the top lid. Also, ensure to seal the valve.
- Press "MANUAL" cooking function and set cooking time to 15 minutes. It will start cooking after a few minutes. Let the pot mix cook under pressure until the timer reads zero.
- Press "Cancel" cooking function and press "Quick release" setting.
- Open the lid and remove the water. Set aside the potato.
- Press "Saute" cooking function.
- Add the oil and potatoes in the pot; cook for 2 minutes to cook well and turn brown.
- Combine the mango powder, salt, and paprika in a bowl and mix well. Coat the wedges with this mixture and serve warm!

Nutrition:

- Calories - 164
- Fat - 6.5g
- Carbs - 25.5g
- Protein - 1.5g

TOMATO AND BASIL SOUP

Serving: 8

Preparation time: 2 minutes

Cooking time: 10 minutes

Ingredients:

- 2 cans whole Roma tomatoes
- ½ cup fresh basil leaves, chopped
- 1 cup vegetable broth
- Salt and pepper to taste
- ¾ cup heavy cream

Directions:

- Place all ingredients except for the heavy cream in the Instant Pot.
- Stir the contents and close the lid.
- Close the lid and press the Manual button.
- Adjust the cooking time to 8 minutes.
- Do quick pressure release.
- Once the lid is open, press the Saute button and stir in the heavy cream.
- Allow simmering for 2 minutes.

Nutrition:

- Calories - 50
- Carbs - 2.8 g
- Protein - 0.86 g
- Fat - 4.31 g

GREEK SUCCOTASH

Serving: 8

Ingredients:

- 1 cup red bell pepper, chopped
- 1 cup zucchini, chopped
- 1 cup eggplant, peeled and cubed
- 2 cups roasted tomatoes, chopped with any liquid
- 1 cup onion, chopped
- 4 cloves garlic, crushed and minced
- ½ cup large Kalamata olives, quartered
- 2 cups white beans, cooked or canned and rinsed
- 1 teaspoon salt
- 1 teaspoon black pepper
- ½ teaspoon nutmeg
- ½ teaspoon oregano
- ½ cup fresh parsley, chopped
- ¼ cup balsamic vinegar
- ¼ cup lemon juice
- 4 cups cooked bulgur
- ½ cup feta cheese, crumbled

Directions:

- Combine the red bell pepper, zucchini, eggplant, tomatoes, onion, garlic, olives, and beans together in a slow cooker.
- Season with salt, black pepper, nutmeg, and oregano. Mix well.
- Cover the slow cooker and cook on LOW for 4 hours.
- Remove the lid and stir in the parsley, balsamic vinegar, lemon juice, and bulgur. Cover and cook an additional 20 minutes.
- Garnish with feta cheese before serving.

Nutrition:

- Calories - 220.8
- Fat - 4.1 g
- Carbs - 39.2 g
- Protein - 9.5 g

SWEET SPICED RIBS

Preparation time: 15-20 minutes

Cooking time: 25 minutes

Serving: 4

Ingredients:

- ½ teaspoon thyme
- ½ teaspoon ground nutmeg
- ½ teaspoon paprika
- 11-ounce pork ribs
- 1 tablespoon honey
- 1 teaspoon olive oil
- 1 tablespoon chicken stock

Directions:

- Rub the ribs with the honey, thyme, ground nutmeg, paprika, and olive oil.
- Let the pork ribs set aside for 5 minutes to marinate.
- Pour the pork ribs with the chicken stock.
- Pour the water and place steamer basket/trivet inside the pot; arrange the ribs over the basket/trivet.
- Close the top lid and seal its valve.
- Press "MEAT" setting. Adjust cooking time to 25 minutes.
- Allow the recipe to cook for the set cooking time.
- After the set cooking time ends, press "CANCEL" and then press "QPR (Quick Pressure Release".
- Instant Pot will quickly release the pressure.
- Open the top lid, add the cooked recipe mix in serving plates.
- Serve and enjoy!

Nutrition:

- Calories - 244
- Fat - 15g
- Carbs - 5.5g
- Protein - 19g

VEGETABLE RICE

Serving: 4-8

Ingredients:

- 2 cups low sodium vegetable stock
- 3 shallots, diced
- 1½ cups frozen vegetables mix
- 2 tablespoons low-sodium soya sauce
- 1 cup long grain brown rice
- Cooking spray
- Salt and pepper

Directions:

- Fry shallots in a non-stick skillet coated with cooking spray until tender, about 2 minutes.
- Coat slow cooker with non-stick cooking spray.
- Place all ingredients in slow cooker.
- Cover and cook for 2 hours on LOW, until rice is tender.

Nutrition:

- Calories - 120
- Fat - 1.0 g
- Carbs - 24.9 g
- Protein - 2.9 g

QUICK CORN ON THE COB

Preparation time: 2 minutes

Cooking time: 3 minutes

Serving: 4

Ingredients:

- 4 ears fresh corn

Directions:

- Pour water into Instant Pot. Place steamer basket over water and arrange corn in the basket.
- Close lid and set cooking time to 3 minutes. Use the quick pressure release method to release steam. Serve corn hot with butter and salt.

Nutrition:

- Calories - 88
- Fat - 1.38 g
- Carbs - 19.07 g
- Protein - 3.34 g

BELL PEPPERS IN WARM SAUCE

Preparation + Cooking time: 20 minutes

Serving: 4

Ingredients:

- 1 medium-sized red bell pepper; chopped
- 1 medium-sized green bell pepper; chopped
- 1 medium-sized yellow bell pepper; chopped
- 1 small chili pepper; finely chopped.
- 1 medium-sized onion; sliced
- 1 small celery stalk; chopped
- 2 tablespoon olive oil
- 1 tablespoon butter
- 2 teaspoon balsamic vinegar
- 2 garlic cloves; finely chopped
- 1/2 cup tomatoes; diced
- 1/4 teaspoon dried thyme; ground.
- 1/2 teaspoon black pepper; ground.
- 1/4 teaspoon ginger powder
- 1/2 teaspoon salt

Directions:

- In a food processor, combine tomatoes, garlic, chili pepper, olive oil, balsamic vinegar, and all spices. Blend until smooth and creamy, Set aside.
- Plug in the instant pot and add butter to the stainless steel insert. Press the "SAUTE" button and melt.
- Add bell peppers and onions. Stir-fry for 3-4 minutes, or until the onions Add celery and pour in the previously blended mixture. Securely lock the lid and set the steam release handle. Press the "MANUAL" button and set the timer for 3 minutes. Cook on "HIGH" pressure
- When you hear the cooker's end signal, perform a quick pressure release by moving the valve to the "VENTING" position.
- Open the pot and a
- serving bowl. Optionally, top with some grated cheese such as parmesan or cheddar cheese.

Nutrition:

- Calories - 179
- Fat - 13.6g
- Carbs - 11.9g
- Protein - 2.2g

BASIL ANGEL HAIR FRITTATA

Serving: 6

Ingredients:

- 2 cups beaten eggs, or egg substitute
- ½ teaspoon salt
- 1 teaspoon black pepper
- 2 cups whole wheat angel hair pasta, cooked
- 1 cup Roma tomatoes, sliced
- 2 cloves garlic, crushed and minced
- 2 cups fresh spinach, torn
- ½ cup fresh basil, torn
- ½ cup fresh grated Parmesan cheese
- Cooking spray

Directions:

- Lightly coat the inside of a slow cooker with vegetable spray.
- Season the beaten egg mixture with salt and black pepper. Layer in the whole wheat angel hair pasta, tomatoes, garlic, spinach, basil, and Parmesan cheese in the slow cooker.
- Pour the egg mixture over and gently stir the ingredients to make sure that the egg mixture goes all the way through to the bottom.
- Cover the slow cooker and cook on HIGH for 2 hours.
- Loosen the edges gently with a spatula before cutting and serving.

Nutrition:

- Calories - 142
- Fat - 2 g
- Carbs - 17 g
- Protein - 13 g

GARLIC CAULIFLOWER MASHED POTATOES

Serving: 6

Ingredients:

- ½ head of cauliflower
- 1 ½ cups water
- 2 large cloves garlic, peeled
- ½ teaspoon salt
- 1 bay leaf
- ½ tablespoon margarine
- Salt and pepper to taste

Directions:

- Cut the cauliflower into florets and place them in the slow cooker.
- Add the water, garlic, salt, and bay leaf.
- Cover, and cook on HIGH for 2-3 hours.
- Remove the cloves of garlic and the bay leaf. Drain the water.

- Add the margarine and let it melt.
- Use a potato masher to make a cauliflower puree.
- Season with salt and pepper to taste.

Nutrition:

- Calories - 96.4
- Fat - 5.9 g
- Carbs - 10.4 g
- Protein - 3.2 g

BALSAMIC PORK WITH SHIITAKE AND BROCCOLI

Preparation + Cooking time: 50 minutes

Serving: 4

Ingredients:

- 2 lbs pork shoulder, boneless
- 2 cups broccoli, cut into florets
- 10 oz shiitake mushrooms, sliced
- 3 tbsp soy sauce
- 2 tbsp oyster sauce
- 3 tbsp balsamic vinegar
- 3 tbsp butter
- 2 cups beef broth
- Spices: 2 bay leaves
- 1 ½ tsp sea salt
- 2 tsp peppercorn

Directions:

- Rinse well the meat and place in the pot. Sprinkle with salt and peppercorn. Pour in the broth and one cup of water. Add bay leaves and seal the lid. Set the steam release handle and press the "MANUAL" button.
- Cook for 25 minutes on high pressure.
- When done, perform a quick pressure release and open the lid. Remove half of the remaining liquid and add broccoli, shiitake, soy sauce, oyster sauce, balsamic vinegar, and butter.
- Seal the lid again and continue to cook for another 8 minutes on the "MANUAL" mode.
- When done, release the pressure naturally and serve immediately.

Nutrition:

- Calories - 483
- Fat - 17.6g
- Carbs - 11.7g
- Protein - 65g

EASY-TO-PREPARE BROCCOLI

Preparation + Cooking time: 15 minutes

Serving: 4

Ingredients:

- 4 cups broccoli florets
- 6 minced garlic cloves
- 1 tbsp. butter
- 1 tbsp. fresh lime juice
- Salt, to taste

Directions:

- In the bottom of Instant Pot, arrange a steamer basket and pour 1 cup of water.
- Place the broccoli into the steamer basket.
- Secure the lid and place the pressure valve to "Seal" position.
- Select "MANUAL" and cook under "Low Pressure" for about 10 minutes.
- Select the "Cancel" and carefully do a "Natural" release.
- Remove the lid and Remove water from the pot and with paper towels, pat dry.
- Place the butter in the Instant Pot and select "Saute". Then add the garlic and cook for about 30 seconds.
- Add the broccoli and lime juice and cook for about 30 seconds.
- Stir in salt and cook for about 1 minute.
- Select the "Cancel" and serve.

Nutrition:

- Calories - 64
- Fat - 3.2g
- Carbs - 1.9g
- Protein - 2.9g

SOUPS AND STEWS

CHICKEN KALE SOUP

Preparation + Cooking time: 5 minutes

Serving: 4

Ingredients:

- 2 cups Chicken Breast (cooked)
- 12 oz Kale (frozen)
- 1 medium Onion (diced)
- 4 cups Chicken Broth
- ½ tsp Cinnamon
- 1 pinch Ground Cloves
- 2 tsp Garlic (minced)

- 1 tsp Ground Black Pepper
- 1 tsp Salt

Directions:

- Place all ingredients in the Instant Pot.
- Place and lock the lid and manually set the cooking time to 5 minutes at high pressure.
- When done let naturally release the pressure for 10 minutes and then quick release it.
- Adjust the seasonings if needed and serve warm.

Nutrition:

- Calories - 143
- Fat - 2g
- Carbs - 4g
- Protein - 23g

CREAMY CHORIZO POTATO SOUP

Serving: 3

Ingredients:

- 4-5 oz spicy chorizo, chopped into chunks
- ½ Tbsp oil
- ½ Tbsp minced garlic
- ½ tsp dried thyme
- 2 cups chicken stock
- Salt to taste
- 7 1/2 oz potatoes, peeled, cubed
- 1 small onion, chopped
- ½ tsp cumin powder
- 2 bay leaves
- ½ cup full fat milk
- 1 green onion, sliced

Directions:

- Place a skillet over medium heat. Add oil and heat. Add onion and saute until Stir in garlic and saute until aromatic.
- Stir in chorizo and saute until fat begins to release.
- Stir in potatoes. Add thyme and cumin powder. Saute until aromatic and turn off the heat.
- Stir in stock and bay leaves.
- Cover and cook for 5-6 hours on low or until potatoes are cooked.
- Add milk and salt. Cover and cook for another 30 minutes.
- Ladle into soup bowls. Sprinkle green onion on top and serve.

Nutrition:

- Calories - 248

PUCHERO A LA VALENCIA (SPANISH STEW)

Serving: 8

Preparation time: 2 minutes

Cooking time: 30 minutes

Ingredients:

- 1 daikon radish, peeled and sliced thickly
- 1 rutabaga, peeled and sliced thickly
- 2 carrots, peeled and cut into chunks
- 2 stalks of celery, chopped
- 1 bunch artichoke hearts, trimmed and sliced
- 2 large beef bones
- ¼ cup chicken breasts, cut into chunks
- 1-pound beef stew meat, cut into chunks
- A pinch of saffron
- 1 can garbanzos beans, drained and rinsed
- 4 cups water

Directions:

- Place all ingredients in the Instant Pot.
- Close the lid and press the Manual button.
- Adjust the cooking time to 30 minutes.
- Do natural pressure release.

Nutrition:

- Calories - 469
- Carbs - 8.4g
- Protein - 8.6g
- Fat - 44.9g

BASIC CAULIFLOWER SOUP

Serving: 3

Ingredients:

- 1/2 cauliflower head, chopped
- 1 Tbsp butter
- 1/4 onion, diced
- 2 cups low sodium vegetable broth
- 1/2 tsp sea salt
- 1/2 tsp pepper
- Zest of 1/4 lemon

Directions:

- Combine the vegetable broth, sea salt, pepper, and onion in the slow cooker.
- Add the chopped cauliflower and butter.
- Cover and cook for 5 hours on low.
- Turn off the slow cooker and let stand for 10 minutes to cool slightly. Blend the soup with a blender until smooth, then stir in the zest and reheat in the slow cooker.
- Serve warm.

Nutrition:

- Calories - 98

BEEF SOUP WITH BARLEY

Serving: 8

Ingredients:

- 2 pounds boneless beef chuck steak, cut into 2-inch pieces
- 4 cloves garlic, minced
- 1 onion, chopped
- 2 pounds baby carrots
- 1 cup white mushrooms, sliced
- 2 stalks celery, chopped
- 1 cup pearl barley, uncooked
- 1 48-ounce carton beef broth, reduced sodium and fat free
- 1 8-ounce can tomato sauce
- 1/8 cup Worcestershire sauce
- Salt and pepper
- Fresh parsley, chopped, for garnish

Directions:

- Put all the ingredients, except parsley, in the slow cooker. Stir.
- Cook for 8-9 hours on LOW or for 4 hours on HIGH.
- Serve garnished with chopped parsley

Nutrition:

- Calories - 275
- Fat - 6 g
- Carbs - 28 g
- Protein - 28 g

COZY CHICKEN AND CORN CHOWDER

Serving: 8

Ingredients:

- 1 pound boneless skinless chicken thighs, cut into 1-inch pieces
- 2 large red potatoes, diced

- 1 onion, diced
- 3 carrots, peeled and diced
- 2 stalks celery, diced
- 2 cups corn kernels
- 2 cups chicken broth
- 2 cups milk
- 3 cloves garlic, minced
- ½ teaspoon dried thyme
- ½ teaspoon dried oregano
- Pinch of cayenne pepper
- 1 bay leaf
- Salt and pepper
- ½ cup half and half
- 2 tablespoons cornstarch
- 2 tablespoons unsalted butter
- 5 slices bacon, cooked and diced
- 2 tablespoons chopped fresh chives

Directions:

- Arrange the chicken, potatoes, onion, carrots, celery, corn, chicken broth, milk, garlic, and bay leaf in the slow cooker. Season with thyme, oregano, and cayenne pepper.
- Cover and cook for 7-8 hours on LOW or for 3-4 hours on HIGH.
- Whisk the cornstarch and half and half together in a bowl.
- Thirty minutes before cooking is complete, stir in the half and half mixture. Add butter.
- Cook 10 to 15 minutes more or until the soup is thick and creamy.
- Serve garnished with bacon and chives.

Nutrition:

- Calories - 293
- Fat - 13 g
- Carbs - 26 g
- Protein - 19 g

OXTAIL STEW

Serving: 2

Preparation time: 20 minutes

Cooking time: 10 hours

Ingredients:

- 2 lb oxtail, chopped
- 10 tomatoes, diced
- 4 tsp paprika

Directions:

- Place oxtail in the crockpot with water filling up to half the pot.
- Cover and cook for 10 hours on low.
- When cooked, Stew for 15 minutes.

Nutrition:

- Calories - 456
- Fat - 29 g
- Carbs - 7 g
- Protein - 37 g

CRAB AND BELL PEPPER SOUP

Serving: 6

Ingredients:

- 2 medium bell peppers, diced
- 3 medium green onions, chopped
- 3 medium carrots, sliced thinly
- 3 Tbsp water
- 1/6 tsp sea salt
- 1/6 tsp cayenne pepper
- 1 large garlic clove, minced
- 1 1/2 cups fat free half and half
- 18 oz canned coconut milk
- 9 oz canned crabmeat, drained, cartilage removed
- 2/3 cup chopped fresh cilantro
- 1 1/2 Tbsp freshly squeezed lime juice
- 3 tsp Sucanat or xylitol
- 1 1/2 tsp grated peeled ginger root
- 1 large lime, sliced into 6 wedges

Directions:

- Coat the slow cooker with nonstick cooking spray.
- Scatter the bell pepper on the bottom, followed by the carrots, green onion, water, garlic, salt, and cayenne.
- Mix well.
- Cover and cook for 3 hours and 30 minutes on low or for 1 hour and 45 minutes on high.
- Increase heat to high and add the half and half, coconut milk, crabmeat, cilantro, Sucanat or xylitol, ginger root, and lime juice.
- Mix well.
- Cover and cook for an additional 15 minutes.
- Serve with lime wedges.

Nutrition:

- Calories - 181

TEXAS BEEF CHILI

Serving: 8

Preparation time: 5 minutes

Cooking time: 20 minutes

Ingredients:

- 1-pound ground beef
- 1 green bell pepper, seeded and chopped
- 1 onion, diced
- 4 large carrots, chopped finely
- 1 can crushed tomatoes
- 1 teaspoon onion powder
- 1 tablespoon parsley, chopped
- 1 tablespoon Worcestershire sauce
- 4 teaspoons chili powder
- 1 teaspoon paprika
- 1 teaspoon cu minutes
- 1 teaspoon garlic powder
- Salt and pepper

Directions:

- Press the Saute button on the Instant Pot.
- Add in the ground beef and add in the bell peppers and onions until fragrant.
- Pour in the rest of the ingredients.
- Close the lid and press the Manual button.
- Adjust the cooking time to 15 minutes.
- Do natural pressure release.

Nutrition:

- Calories - 267
- Carbs - 23.7g
- Protein - 21.3g
- Fat - 9.9g

CAJUN SAUSAGE AND WHITE BEAN SOUP

Serving: 6

Ingredients:

- 1 pound dried Great Northern beans
- ½ pound Cajun andouille sausage, sliced
- 1 large onion, chopped
- 2 stalks celery, chopped
- 4 sprigs fresh thyme
- 8 cups chicken broth, low-sodium
- 8 cups collard greens, leaves only, cut to 1-inch pieces

- 1 tablespoon red wine vinegar
- Salt and pepper

Directions:

- Set aside the last 3 ingredients.
- Place the beans, sausage, onion, celery, thyme, and chicken broth in the slow cooker and stir.
- Cover and cook for 7 to 8 hours on LOW or for 4 to 5 hours on HIGH.
- Beans should be tender.
- Remove the thyme stems and drop in the collard greens. Cover and cook 15 minutes longer or until the greens are tender.
- Add the vinegar, and salt and pepper to taste.

Nutrition:

- Calories - 393
- Fat - 8 g
- Carbs - 51 g
- Protein - 30 g

EASY BEEF SOUP

Preparation + Cooking time: 50 minutes

Serving: 3

Ingredients:

- For soup: 1 lb beef stew meat
- 1 small onion, sliced
- 1 cup kale, chopped
- 2 tbsp butter
- 4 cups beef broth
- 2 garlic cloves, crushed
- Spices: 1 tsp cayenne pepper
- ¼ tsp black pepper, freshly ground
- ½ tsp salt

Directions:

- Plug in the instant pot and grease the inner pot with butter. Press the "Saute" button and heat up.
- Add onions and garlic. Cook for 3 minutes, or until Pour in the broth and season with salt, pepper, and cayenne pepper.
- Seal the lid and set the steam release handle.
- Press the "MANUAL" button and set the timer for 25 minutes on high pressure.
- When done, perform a quick steam release and open the lid. Stir in the chopped kale and seal the lid again.
- Let it sit for about 10-15 minutes before serving.

Nutrition:

- Calories - 423
- Fat - 19g
- Carbs - 5.5g
- Protein - 53.5g

KETO STEWED SCOTCH EGG

Preparation + Cooking time: 28 minutes

Serving: 8

Ingredients:

- 2lbs 20% fat pork mince, ground, salted and peppered
- 8 eggs
- 2 cups almond meal
- 2 cups tomato sauce
- 2 tbsp. coconut oil
- 1oz mixed herbs
- dipping sauces

Directions:

- Put the eggs into your Instant Pot and add water to cover, plus half an inch, if your limit allows.
- Depending on your model of Instant Pot, either set to Eggs, or set to Stew and cook for 6 minutes
- Remove the eggs and put them in ice water.
- As the eggs chill, split the mince down into 8 balls and flatten them out.
- Combine the almonds, herbs, and half a tbsp. of coconut oil.
- Once cool, peel the eggs.
- Place one in each flattened sausage.
- Roll the sausage into a ball around the egg.
- Roll in almond meal and coconut oil mix.
- Clear out your Instant Pot and add the remaining oil.
- Leaving the top open, cook the eggs on high, rolling to ensure even browning.
- Add the tomato sauce and simmer for 5 minutes.

Nutrition:

- Calories - 300
- Fat - 34g
- Carbs - 11g
- Protein - 32g

STEWED BEEF

Preparation + Cooking time: 30 minutes

Serving: 6

Ingredients:

- 3 lbs. diced beef rump
- 1 marrow bone
- 2 cups tomato
- 1 cup chopped red onion
- 1 cup chopped spring onion
- 2 tbsp. olive oil
- 2 tbsp. oregano
- 2 bay leaves
- salt and pepper to taste

Directions:

- Put your Instant Pot on High and warm the oil in it.
- Add the beef, salt and pepper, and red onion.
- Soften 5 minutes.
- Add the remaining ingredients.
- Seal and cook on Stew for 20 minutes.
- Release the pressure slowly.
- Discard the bay leaves and bone.
- Shred the beef and onions in the sauce.

Nutrition:

- Calories - 340
- Fat - 20g
- Carbs - 11g
- Protein - 33g

BEEF RAGOUT

Preparation + Cooking time: 25 minutes

Serving: 6

Ingredients:

- For ragout: 2 lbs beef stew meat
- 1 cup cherry tomatoes, chopped
- 1 cup cauliflower, finely chopped
- 3 small onions, finely chopped
- 2 tbsp balsamic vinegar
- 1 celery rib, thinly sliced
- 3 tbsp olive oil
- 2 tbsp butter
- Spices: 1 tsp salt

- 1 tbsp smoked paprika
- ½ tsp black pepper

Directions:

- Rinse the meat under cold running water and pat dry with a kitchen paper.
- Cut into 1-inch thick pieces and set aside.
- Plug in the instant pot and grease the bottom of the inner pot with olive oil. Rub the meat with salt and make the bottom layer. Add cherry tomatoes and cauliflower and season with salt, smoked paprika, and black pepper. Sprinkle with onions and pour in the vinegar and beef broth.
- Top with celery rib and seal the lid.
- Set the steam release handle to the "Sealing" position and press the "Meat" button.
- Cook for 20 minutes on high pressure.
- When done, press the "Cancel" button to turn off the heat and release the pressure naturally.
- Open the lid and stir in the butter.
- Let it chill for a while before serving.

Nutrition:

- Calories - 400
- Fat - 20.4g
- Carbs - 4g
- Protein - 46.9g

FRENCH ONION SOUP

Serving: 6

Ingredients:

- 2 Tbsp unsalted butter
- 1 bay leaf
- ½ Tbsp sugar
- 1 Tbsp vinegar
- ½ tsp black pepper
- ¾ cup shredded gruyere cheese
- 2 sprigs thyme
- 2 ½ lb large sweet onions, halved, thinly sliced
- 3 cups unsalted vegetable stock or beef stock
- 1 tsp kosher salt or to taste
- 12 slices whole grain French bread baguette, toasted

Directions:

- Add butter, thyme sprigs, onions, and bay leaf into the slow cooker. Sprinkle sugar all over it. Here sugar is necessary to brown the onions.
- Cover and cook on high for 8 hours. Stir a couple of times during this time.
- Discard thyme sprigs and bay leaf.
- Add stock, vinegar, salt and pepper.

- Stir well.
- Cover and cook for 30 minutes on high.
- Ladle into individual ovenproof soup bowls.
- Set the oven to broil and preheat the oven.
- Place baguette slices on a baking sheet. Place baking sheet in the oven and broil for 30-60 seconds. Flip sides and broil for 30-60 seconds or until the way you like it toasted.
- Place toasted bread slices on the top of the soup. Sprinkle cheese over the bread slices.
- Broil in the oven for 2 minutes or until the cheese melts and is light brown.
- Serve immediately.

Nutrition:

- Calories - 240

RABBIT STEW

Cooking time: 5 hours

Serving: 6

Ingredients:

- Rabbit - 3 lbs., cut into pieces
- Uncured bacon - ½ lb., cubed
- Butter - 2 tbsp.
- Dry white wine - 2 cups
- Large sweet onion - 1, chopped
- Bay leaves - 2
- Rosemary - 1 large sprig
- Salt and pepper to taste
- Method
- Add the cubed bacon and butter in a skillet.
- Add the sliced onion and cook for 5 minutes. Then remove the onion and leave the fat in the pan.
- Add the rabbit and saute on high heat until browned. Pour in the wine and let it simmer for a couple of minutes.
- Add everything from the pan to the Crock-Pot. Add bay leaves, rosemary, salt, and pepper.
- Cover and cook on low heat for 5 hours.

Nutrition:

- Calories - 517
- Fat - 32g
- Carbs - 2g
- Protein - 36g

SWISS CHARD STEM SOUP

Serving: 6

Preparation time: 3 minutes

Cooking time: 4 minutes

Ingredients:

- 8 cups Swiss Chard stems, diced
- 3 leeks, chopped
- 1 celeriac, peeled and diced
- 1 potato, peeled and diced
- 1 ½ cups chicken stock
- 1 cup coconut milk
- Salt and pepper to taste

Directions:

- Place all ingredients in the Instant Pot.
- Give a good stir to combine everything.
- Close the lid and press the Manual button.
- Adjust the cooking time to 4 minutes.
- Do natural pressure release.

Nutrition:

- Calories - 200
- Carbs - 23.9g
- Protein - 5.4g
- Fat - 10.6g

POWER HOUSE GREEN SOUP

Serving: 4

Ingredients:

- 8 ounces spinach, roughly chopped
- 1 bunch kale, trimmed with stems removed and chopped
- 1 onion, diced
- Salt and pepper
- ¼ cup fresh basil, chopped
- 4 cups vegetable broth

Directions:

- In the slow cooker, add spinach, kale, onion, and broth. Season generously with salt and pepper
- Cover and cook for
- 6 hours on LOW or
- 3 hours on HIGH.
- Blend the soup with a hand held blender until smooth.
- Add chopped basil.

- Taste and add more salt or pepper if required.

Nutrition:

- Calories - 89
- Fat - 3 g
- Carbs - 2.8 g
- Protein - 0.9 g

FISH AND SEAFOOD

COCONUT CLAMS

Serving: 2

Ingredients:

- ¼ cup coconut milk
- 2 eggs, whisked
- 1 tablespoon olive oil
- 10 ounces canned clams, chopped
- 1 green bell pepper, chopped
- 1 yellow onion, chopped
- Salt and black pepper to taste

Directions:

- Combine all the ingredients in the slow cooker.
- Cover, and cook on LOW for 6 hours.
- Divide among serving bowls or plates and enjoy!

Nutrition:

- Calories - 271
- Fat - 4.2 g
- Carbs - 16 g
- Protein - 7.6 g

SHRIMP AND TOMATO CASSEROLE

Preparation + Cooking time: 30 minutes

Serving: 4

Ingredients:

- 1 ½ pounds Shrimp, peeled and deveined
- 1 ½ pounds Tomatoes, chopped
- 2 tbsp. Olive Oil
- ½ cup Veggie Broth

- ¼ cup chopped Cilantro
- 2 tbsp. Lime Juice
- 1 Jalapeno, diced
- 1 Onion, diced
- 1 cup shredded Cheddar Cheese
- 1 tsp minced Garlic

Directions:

- Heat the olive oil in your Instant Pot on SAUTE.
- Add onion and cook for 3 minutes.
- Add garlic and saute for additional 30-60 seconds.
- Stir in the broth, cilantro, and tomatoes.
- Close the lid and cook on HIGH for 9 minutes.
- Do a natural pressure release.
- Add shrimp and cook on HIGH for 2 more minutes.
- Release the pressure quickly and stir in cheddar,
- Serve and enjoy!

Nutrition:

- Calories - 300
- Fat - 16g
- Carbs - 8g
- Protein - 22g

INDIAN STYLE PRAWNS AND PEAS

Serving: 2

Ingredients:

- 100 g frozen peas
- 1/2 lb raw king prawns
- 100 g cherry tomatoes, halved
- 1/2 tsp sunflower oil
- 1 onion, sliced
- 2 garlic cloves, crushed
- 1/2 tsp ground ginger
- 1 Tbsp chopped fresh cilantro or coriander
- 1 1/2 Tbsp curry paste
- 1/2 cup sieved tomatoes
- sea salt
- Pepper

Directions:

- Combine the peas, tomatoes, onion, garlic, and sunflower oil in the slow cooker. Add the ground ginger, curry paste, and sieved tomatoes.
- Place the prawns inside and season with a dash of sea salt and pepper.

- Cover and cook or 2 hours on low, or until the peas are tender and the prawns are cooked through. Before serving, top with chopped coriander. Best served with black, red or cauliflower rice.

Nutrition:

- Calories - 269

EASY ORIENTAL TUNA

Serving: 6

Ingredients:

- 6 green onions
- 3 tsp soy sauce
- 1 large garlic clove, minced
- 1 1/2 lb tuna steak, patted dry and sliced into 6 pieces
- 1 1/2 tsp minced peeled ginger root
- 3/4 tsp chili sauce

Directions:

- Place the green onions in the slow cooker in a single layer. Place the tuna steaks on top.
- Combine the soy sauce, garlic, ginger root, and chili sauce in a small bowl, then pour on top of the fish.
- Cover and cook for 1 hour and 30 minutes on high.

Nutrition:

- Calories - 137

WHITE FISH STEW

Preparation + Cooking time: 20 minutes

Serving: 6

Ingredients:

- 1 Onion, diced
- 1 Carrot, sliced
- 2 Celery Stalks, diced
- 1 cup Heavy Cream
- 1 pound White Fish Fillets
- 3 cups Fish Broth
- 1 cup chopped Broccoli
- 1 cup chopped Cauliflower
- 1 cup chopped Kale
- 2 tbsp. Butter
- Salt and Pepper, to taste

Directions:

- Melt the butter in your Instant Pot on SAUTE.
- Saute the onions for 3 minutes.
- Stir all of the ingredients, except for the cream.
- Close the lid and select MANUAL.
- Cook on HIGH for 5 minutes.
- Do a natural pressure release.
- Stir in the heavy cream.
- Discard the bay leaf and serve.

Nutrition:

- Calories - 165
- Fat - 13g
- Carbs - 5g
- Protein - 24g

HONEY-GLAZED SHRIMPS

Serving: 4

Ingredients:

- ¼ cup sesame oil
- ½ pound green beans
- 3 pounds shrimp
- Salt, to taste
- Pepper, to taste
- ½ cup orange juice
- 2 teaspoons honey
- 2 teaspoons rice wine vinegar
- 4 teaspoons toasted sesame seeds

Directions:

- Turn on the saute mode of the Crock-Pot Express and add oil.
- Add the salt, pepper and green beans.
- Cook until soft.
- Add the juice, honey, rice wine and vinegar.
- Cook for 5 minutes.
- Now add the shrimp, press the STEAM button, and set the pressure to high.
- Set the timer for 4 minutes.
- Serve with a sprinkle of sesame seeds.

Nutrition:

- Calories - 586
- Fat - 21 g
- Carbs - 16 g
- Protein - 76 g

SALMON DIJON WITH DILL

Serving: 6

Ingredients:

- 6 skinless wild caught Alaskan salmon fillets, 5 oz each
- 2 1/4 tsp honey
- 3 Tbsp Dijon mustard
- 12 fresh dill sprigs of 1 1/2 Tbsp dried dill
- 2/3 sweet onion, sliced into rings

Directions:

- Spread out two sheets of aluminum foil on a flat surface to create a cross. Arrange the tilapia in a single layer on the center of one sheet.
- In a bowl, combine the honey and mustard very well, then baste the salmon fillets with this mixture. Arrange the dill sprigs or sprinkle the dried dill on top of the fillets, then arrange the onion rings on top.
- Fold up the aluminum foils and crimp the edges to make packets. Arrange the packets in a slow cooker.
- Cover and cook for 2 hours on low, or until the fish is cooked through.
- Carefully take the packets out of the slow cooker and

Nutrition:

- Calories - 188

TILAPIA FILLETS

Preparation + Cooking time: 40 minutes

Serving: 2

Ingredients:

- 1-pound tilapia fillets; chopped.
- 1 cup fish stock
- 2 tablespoon peanut oil
- 1 spring onion; finely chopped
- 1/4 cup celery leaves; finely chopped.
- 3 tablespoon soy sauce
- 1 tablespoon rice vinegar
- 1 teaspoon garlic powder
- 1 tablespoon fresh ginger; grated
- 1 teaspoon sea salt

Directions:

- In a small bowl, whisk together peanut oil, soy sauce, rice vinegar, ginger, garlic powder, and sea salt. Rub the fish with this mixture and place in a large Ziploc bag. Seal the bag and refrigerate for at least 30 minutes
- Plug in the instant pot and pour in the stock. Remove the fish from the refrigerator and place in the pot along with the marinade. Sprinkle with celery and seal the lid
- Set the steam release handle to the "SEALING" position and press the "MANUAL" button. Set the timer for 6 minutes on high pressure

Nutrition:

- Calories - 348
- Fat - 16.5g
- Carbs - 2.2g
- Protein - 46.6g

SEA BASS IN A TOMATO FETA SAUCE

Preparation + Cooking time: 30 minutes

Serving: 4

Ingredients:

- 4 Sea Bass Fillets
- 1 cup canned diced Tomatoes
- 1/2 cup crumbled Feta Cheese
- 1 tsp chopped Parsley
- 1 tsp chopped Basil
- 1 tsp minced Garlic
- 1 tbsp. Olive Oil
- ¼ tsp salt
- ¼ tsp Pepper
- 1 ½ cups Water

Directions:

- Season the sea bass with salt and pepper.
- Pour the water into the Instant Pot and place the sea bass on the rack.
- Close the lid and cook on HIGH for 5 minutes.
- Heat the oil in the IP on SAUTE.
- Add garlic and cook for 1 minute.
- Add tomatoes and cook for 1 more minute.
- Stir in basil and parsley.
- Add the sea bass and top with feta.
- Cook for 1 minute.
- Serve

Nutrition:

- Calories - 275
- Fat - 8g

- Carbs - 2g
- Protein - 40g

SQUID RINGS WITH POTATO AND SPINACH

Preparation + Cooking time: 35 minutes

Serving: 3

Ingredients:

- 1 lb squid rings, frozen
- 1 lb fresh spinach, torn
- 2 cups cauliflower, roughly chopped
- 4 tbsp extra virgin olive oil
- 2 tbsp lemon juice
- Spices: 1 tsp garlic paste
- 1 tsp dried rosemary, crushed
- 2 thyme sprigs, fresh
- 1 tsp sea salt

Directions:

- Place squid rings in a deep bowl and pour in enough warm water to cover. Let it sit for a while. Set aside.
- Plug in the instant pot and grease the inner pot with two tablespoons of olive oil. Press the "Saute" button and add garlic paste and rosemary. Stir-fry for one minute and then add the spinach. Season with salt and cook for 3-4 minutes or
- until wilted.
- Remove the spinach from the pot and set aside.
- Add the remaining oil to the pot and heat up on the "Saute" mode. Add chopped cauliflower making an even layer. Top with squid rings and drizzle with lemon juice and optionally some more olive oil to taste. Sprinkle with salt, add thyme sprigs, and pour in one cup of water (or fish stock).
- Seal the lid and set the steam release handle to the "Sealing" position. Press the "Fish" button and set the timer for 9 minutes.
- When you hear the cooker's end signal, carefully move the pressure valve to the "Venting" position to release the pressure.
- Open the pot and stir in the spinach. Optionally, season with some more garlic powder or dried thyme.
- Serve

Nutrition:

- Calories - 353
- Fat - 21.5g
- Carbs - 8.9g
- Protein - 29.3g

POACHED SALMON WITH VEGGIES

Serving: 2

Ingredients:

- 1 cup water
- ½ large onion, sliced
- ½ cup dry white wine
- 1 stalk celery, sliced
- 1 leek, cleaned and sliced thinly
- 1 carrot, sliced
- 1 tablespoon lemon juice
- 2 fresh thyme sprigs
- 1 fresh rosemary sprig
- 1 bay leaf
- 1 teaspoon salt
- ¼ teaspoon black pepper
- 2 salmon fillets (6 ounces each
- Lemon wedges for serving

Directions:

- Place all the ingredients except the salmon and lemon wedges in a slow cooker. Mix to combine well.
- Cover and cook for 45 minutes on LOW.
- Now, open the lid and place the salmon fillets carefully in the liquid, making sure they're covered.
- Cover and cook for 45 minutes again. The salmon fillets should be fork tender.
- Serve with lemon wedges.

Nutrition:

- Calories - 272
- Fat - 16 g
- Carbs - 1 g
- Protein - 29 g

STEAMED SALMON RECIPE

Preparation + Cooking time: 15 minutes

Serving: 4

Ingredients:

- 1-pound salmon fillets; sliced into 4 pieces
- 2 lemons; juiced
- 2 cups fish stock
- 1/4 cup Parmesan cheese; freshly grated
- 4 tablespoon butter
- 1 teaspoon white pepper; freshly ground.
- 1 teaspoon smoked salt

Directions:

- Plug in the instant pot and pour in the stock. Drizzle with lemon juice and set the steam basket.
- Rinse the salmon fillets and sprinkle with salt and pepper. Place in the basket and seal the lid.
- Set the steam release handle to the "SEALING" position and press the "MANUAL" button
- Set the timer for 5 minutes.
- When done, perform a quick release and open the lid. Remove the salmon fillets and set asideRemove the stock from the pot.
- Press the "SAUTE" button and melt the butter. Add salmon steaks and cook for 2-3 minutes on each side
- Sprinkle with grated parmesan and serve immediately

Nutrition:

- Calories - 257
- Fat - 18.9g
- Carbs - 0.1g
- Protein - 22.7g

CREAMY MUSSEL SOUP

Preparation + Cooking time: 15 minutes

Serving: 4

Ingredients:

- 2 cups mussels, defrosted
- 1 lb cauliflower, chopped into florets
- 1 cup broccoli, chopped
- 2 cups fish stock
- 1 cup heavy cream
- ¼ cup Parmesan cheese
- 2 tbsp butter, unsalted
- 1 tbsp soy sauce
- Spices: 2 bay leaves
- ½ tsp fresh pepper, ground

Directions:

- Place mussels in a large sieve and rinse thoroughly under cold running water. Drain and place in a deep bowl. Season with pepper and set aside.
- Plug in the instant pot and press the "Saute" button. Add cauliflower and broccoli. Stir well and cook for 5 minutes.
- Now add mussels and pour in the fish stock. Drizzle with soy sauce and add bay leaves.
- Seal the lid and set the steam release handle to the "Sealing" position. Press the "MANUAL" button and set the timer for 5 minutes on high pressure.

- When done, perform a quick release and open the lid. Remove the bay leaves and stir in the heavy cream and Parmesan.
- Chill for a while before serving

Nutrition:

- Calories - 283
- Fat - 20g
- Carbs - 8g
- Protein - 15.9g

COD CHOWDER WITH BACON

Preparation + Cooking time: 25 minutes

Serving: 5

Ingredients:

- 1 lb cod fillets
- 3 cups fish stock
- 2 cups cauliflower, cut into florets
- 1 cup button mushrooms, sliced
- ¼ cup fish sauce
- ½ cup onions, finely chopped
- 1 cup full-fat milk
- 3 tbsp butter
- ¼ cup heavy cream
- 5 bacon slices, chopped

Spices:

- 1 tsp salt
- ½ tsp black pepper, freshly ground
- 1 tsp dried basil

Directions:

- Plug in the instant pot and press the "Saute" button. Grease the inner pot with butter and heat up. Add onions and mushrooms and stir well. Cook for 5 minutes, stirring occasionally.
- Now add the fish stock and cauliflower. Add cod fillets and season with salt, pepper, and basil.
- Add bacon and stir well again.
- Seal the lid and set the steam release handle to the "Sealing" position. Press the "MANUAL" button and set the timer for 8 minutes on high pressure.
- When done, perform a quick pressure release and carefully open the lid.
- Stir in the milk and heavy cream. Drizzle with the fish sauce and chill for a while.
- Serve with some freshly chopped parsley.

Nutrition:

- Calories - 333
- Fat - 20.7g
- Carbs - 5.6g
- Protein - 30.1g

SEASONED LARGE SHRIMP RECIPE

Serving: 5

Ingredients:

- ½ cup chicken broth
- ½ cup white wine (optional; if using white wine, reduce chicken broth to ¼ cup)
- 2 tablespoons olive oil
- 2 teaspoons garlic, chopped
- 2 teaspoons parsley, minced
- 1 pound large raw shrimp, thawed

Directions:

- Place all the ingredients (except the shrimp) in your crockpot and mix.
- Place the shrimp into the mixture and cook everything on LOW for 2½ hours.
- Remove the shrimp and place in a bowl.
- Stir the mixture one last time and then pour over the shrimp.
- Serve and enjoy.

Nutrition:

- Calories - 130
- Fat - 1 g
- Carbs - 15 g
- Protein - 4 g

PARSLEY HALIBUT

Preparation time: 10 minutes

Cooking time: 4.5 hours

Serving: 5

Ingredients:

- 5 halibut fillets
- ¼ cup fresh parsley
- 1 teaspoon salt
- ½ teaspoon sage
- 1/3 cup butter

Directions:

- Put the fresh parsley in the blender and blend until smooth.
- Then add salt, sage, and butter.
- Blend the mixture until homogenous and Add halibut fillets and close the lid.
- Cook the fish on Low for 4.5 hours.

Nutrition:

- Calories - 428
- Fat - 19
- Carbs - 0.2
- Protein - 60.7

SOUR KING SCALLOPS RECIPE

Preparation + Cooking time: 20 minutes

Serving: 4

Ingredients:

- 5 king scallops; fresh
- 2 tablespoon olive oil
- 1 medium-sized onion; finely chopped
- 1/4 cup apple cider vinegar
- 3 tablespoon butter
- 1 tablespoon fresh lemon juice
- 1 cup fish stock
- 1/2 teaspoon garlic powder
- 1/2 teaspoon white pepper; freshly ground.
- 1 teaspoon salt

Directions:

- Plug in the instant pot and grease the inner pot with olive oil. Heat up and add onions. Cook for 3-4 minutes, or until Pour in the stock and apple cider vinegar. Add scallops and gently simmer for 5 minutes.
- Season with salt, garlic powder, and white pepper. Give it a good stir and press the "CANCEL" button.
- Seal the lid and set the steam release handle. Press the "MANUAL" button and set the timer for 8 minutes.
- When done; perform a quick pressure release and open the lid
- Stir in the butter and sprinkle with lemon juice. Serve and enjoy.

Nutrition:

- Calories - 389
- Fat - 31.3g
- Carbs - 1.4g
- Protein - 27.1g

COCONUT CLAM CHOWDER

Preparation time: 15 minutes

Cooking time: 3 hours

Serving: 2

Ingredients:

- 3 oz celery stalk
- ¼ cup cauliflower florets
- 1 cup clams
- 1 cayenne pepper, chopped
- 1 teaspoon salt
- ½ teaspoon ground black pepper
- 2 tablespoon lemon juice
- 3 tablespoons coconut cream
- 1 cup of water
- 2 tablespoons fresh parsley, chopped

Directions:

- Chop celery stalk and put it in the crockpot.
- Add cauliflower florets, cayenne pepper, salt, ground black pepper, water, and fresh parsley.
- Close the lid and cook the ingredients for 2.5 hours on High.
- After this, add lemon juice, clams, and coconut cream. Stir the chowder well.
- Cook the chowder for 30 minutes on High. The clams in the cooked chowder are opened.

Nutrition:

- Calories - 155
- Fat - 6.9
- Carbs - 7.5
- Protein - 16

CHICKEN AND POULTRY

CHICKEN, BEANS AND CORN RECIPE

Serving: 6

Ingredients:

- 2 pounds boneless chicken breasts, fresh or frozen
- 1 can (15 ounces black beans, drained, rinsed
- 1 can (15 ounces) corn, drained, rinsed
- 1 jar (16 ounces) salsa verde (or regular salsa)
- 8 ounces cream cheese

- Optional side dishes: rice, noodles

Directions:

- Cover the bottom of a slow cooker with the chicken, and then top with the beans, corn and salsa.
- Cook everything on LOW for 6 hours.
- Place the block of cream cheese on top of the chicken mixture, re-cover the slow cooker, and let sit for 30 minutes.

Nutrition:

- Calories - 145
- Fat - 2 g
- Carbs - 5 g
- Protein - 26 g

DUCK BREAST WITH PROSCIUTTO

Preparation + Cooking time: 50 minutes

Serving: 4

Ingredients:

- 1 lb duck breasts
- 1 shallot, finely chopped
- 2 garlic cloves, crushed
- ½ cup duck fat
- 4 cups chicken broth
- 7 oz prosciutto, chopped
- 2 tbsp fresh parsley, finely chopped
- 3 tbsp apple cider vinegar
- 1 cup cremini mushrooms
- 1 tbsp orange zest

Spices:

- 1 tsp sea salt
- ½ tsp white pepper, freshly ground

Directions:

- Plug in the instant pot and press the "Saute" button. Add duck fat and slowly melt, stirring constantly.
- Now add shallots and garlic. Give it a good stir and cook for 2-3 minutes. Add mushrooms and continue to cook until the liquid has evaporated.
- Finally, add prosciutto and stir well. Briefly brown on all sides and press the "Cancel" button.
- Add the meat in the pot and pour in the broth. Sprinkle with spices and orange zest.
- Pour in the cider and seal the lid.

- Set the steam release handle to the "Sealing" position and press the "MANUAL" button.
- Set the timer for 20 minutes on high pressure.
- When done, release the pressure naturally and carefully open the lid. Sprinkle with parsley and let it sit covered for about 10 minutes before serving.

Nutrition:

- Calories - 496
- Fat - 34.3g
- Carbs - 3.5g
- Protein - 40.9g

GLAZED DUCK BREAST

Preparation + Cooking time: 50 minutes

Serving: 2

Ingredients:

- 1 lb. duck breast, chopped into bite-sized pieces
- 1 tbsp. olive oil
- 3 cups chicken broth
- 1 tbsp. Dijon mustard
- 1 tsp honey
- ¼ cup apple cider vinegar

Spices:

- 1 tsp salt
- ½ tsp pepper
- 1 tsp garlic powder

Directions:

- Remove the meat from the refrigerator about one hour before cooking.
- Rub the meat with onion powder and place in your instant pot along with the chicken broth. Seal the lid and press the "MEAT" button. When you hear the cooker's end signal, perform a quick release and open the lid. Remove the meat from the pot along with the broth.
- Press the "SAUTE" button and grease the stainless steel insert with oil. Add apple cider, Dijon, and honey. Sprinkle with salt and pepper and cook for 3-4 minutes.
- Add the meat and coat well.
- Serve immediately.

Nutrition:

- Calories - 398
- Fat - 15g
- Carbs - 4.7g
- Protein - 55.7g

CHICKEN MOLE TACOS

Serving: 4 (3 oz chicken with 2 tortillas and ½ cup sauce

Ingredients:

- 7 1/2 ounces unsalted, diced tomatoes with its juice
- ¼ cup almonds, toasted
- 1 oz Ancho chilies, stemmed, deseeded
- ½ Tbsp dried oregano
- ¼ tsp ground cinnamon
- A pinch ground cloves
- ½ ounce Mexican chocolate, grated or 1 Tbsp bitter-sweet chocolate chips
- ½ cup stout or chicken broth
- 2 Tbsp sesame seeds, toasted, + extra to garnish
- 2 cloves garlic, crushed
- Salt to taste
- 1/8 tsp ground allspice
- 4 bone-in chicken thighs, skinless, trimmed
- 8 corn tortillas, warmed
- Lime wedges to serve
- Radish slices to serve
- Cooking spray

Directions:

- Add tomatoes, almonds, beer or broth, garlic, sesame seeds, salt, oregano, allspice, cinnamon and cloves into a blender and blend until smooth.
- Spray the inside of the slow cooker with cooking spray. Pour the blended sauce into the slow cooker. Place chicken in it and stir.
- Cover and cook for 3 hours on high or 6 hours on low.
- Remove chicken with a slotted spoon and place on your cutting board. When cool enough to handle, shred the meat.
- Add chocolate and mix well.
- Serve chicken over tortillas. Sprinkle sesame seeds. Garnish with radish and serve with lime wedges.

Nutrition:

- Calories - 460

SLOW COOKER FRENCH CHICKEN

Preparation time: 20 minutes

Cooking time: 4 hour

Serving: 6

Ingredients:

- 1 can onion soup
- 1-pound chicken drumsticks
- 7 oz baby carrot
- 4 oz celery stalk
- 1 teaspoon sage
- ¼ teaspoon tarragon
- ½ teaspoon ground coriander
- 1 tablespoon vinegar
- ¼ cup white wine
- ½ teaspoon oregano

Directions:

- Put the chicken drumsticks in the slow cooker bowl.
- Sprinkle with the sage and tarragon. Add the ground coriander and vinegar along with the white wine and oregano. Wash the baby carrots carefully and cut them into the halves.
- Chop the celery stalk. Add the baby carrot halves and chopped celery stalk in the slow cooker bowl.
- Add the canned onion soup and close the lid. Cook the dish for 4 hours on HIGH.
- Serve hot!

Nutrition:

- Calories - 182
- Fat - 9.2
- Carbs - 8.79
- Protein - 15

ORANGE CHICKEN MEAL

Preparation time: 5 minutes

Cooking time: 17 minutes

Serving: 2-3

Ingredients:

- 2 tablespoons brown sugar
- 1/4 cup chicken stock
- 1 pound chicken breast, skinless and boneless, cut into small pieces
- Juice 1 orange or more to taste
- 1 tablespoon tomato ketchup
- 2 tablespoons flour
- 1 tablespoon coconut oil

Directions:

- Coat the chicken with the flour in a bowl.
- Set aside.

- Take your Instant Pot and open the top lid.
- Press "SAUTE" mode.
- Add the oil and heat it; stir-cook the chicken until evenly brown for 2-3 minutes.
- Add remaining ingredients; gently stir.
- Close the top lid and seal the pressure valve.
- Press "MANUAL" setting with 15 minutes of cooking time and "HIGH" pressure mode.
- Press "QPR" function to release the pressure.
- Open the lid; Enjoy!

Nutrition:

- Calories - 394
- Fat - 12g
- Carbs - 24g
- Sodium - 324mg
- Protein - 46g

PORTABELLA CHICKEN MEATLOAF

Serving: 4

Ingredients:

- 2 cups portabella mushrooms, chopped
- 1 tablespoon butter
- ½ teaspoon salt
- ½ teaspoon black pepper
- ½ cup ground almond flour
- ½ cup Parmesan cheese, freshly grated
- 1 ½ pounds ground chicken
- 1 egg
- ½ cup yellow onion, diced
- ½ cup celery, diced
- 2 cloves garlic, crushed and minced
- 1 tablespoon fresh oregano
- ¼ cup fresh basil, chopped

Directions:

- Melt the butter in a skillet over medium heat.
- Add the mushrooms, season with salt and black pepper, and saute for 1-2 minutes. Remove the skillet from the heat and allow it to cool.
- Place the ground chicken in a bowl, and stir in the mushroom mixture.
- Next, add the egg, onion, celery, garlic, oregano, and basil. Mix the meat mixture until all the ingredients are well incorporated.
- Line a slow cooker with aluminum foil to make removing the meatloaf easier.
- Press the meat mixture gently into the bottom of the slow cooker and shape as desired.
- Cover and cook on low for 8 hours.

Nutrition:

- Calories - 486.4
- Fat - 31.9 g
- Carbs - 8 g
- Protein - 42.2 g

CHICKEN CREAM SOUP

Preparation time: 15 minutes

Cooking time: 9 hours

Serving: 10

Ingredients:

- 18 oz chicken
- 8 cups water
- 1 tablespoon salt
- ½ cup heavy cream
- 1 teaspoon ground black pepper
- 1 teaspoon turmeric
- 5 oz Monterey cheese
- 1/3 cup fresh dill, chopped
- 2 potatoes, peeled
- 1 teaspoon chili flakes

Directions:

- Chop the chicken roughly and put it in the slow cooker.
- Add water and salt.
- After this, add the ground black pepper, turmeric and the chili flakes. Chopped peeled potatoes and add them in the slow cooker too.
- Close the lid and cook the mixture for 9 hours on LOW. Remove the chicken from the slow cooker and shred it. Blend the slow cooker mixture with the help of the hand blender.
- When you get a smooth soup, it is done.
- Add Monterey cheese and chopped fresh dill.
- Return the shredded chicken to the slow cooker and close the lid. Cook the soup for 1 hour on HIGH or until the soup is smooth and the cheese is melted.
- Serve the soup hot. Enjoy!

Nutrition:

- Calories - 207
- Fat - 10.8
- Carbs - 13.96
- Protein - 14

CASHEW CHICKEN

Preparation time: 10 minutes

Cooking time: 4 hours

Serving: 6

Ingredients:

- 1 and ½ pound chicken breast, boneless, skinless and cubed
- 1 tablespoon coconut oil
- 3 tablespoons coconut aminos
- 2 tablespoons tapioca flour
- Black pepper to the taste
- 1 tablespoon unsweetened ketchup
- 2 tablespoons white vinegar
- 1 teaspoon ginger, grated
- 2 tablespoons palm sugar
- ½ cup cashews, chopped
- 2 garlic cloves, minced
- 1 green onion, chopped

Directions:

- Put chicken pieces in a bowl, season with black pepper, add tapioca flour and toss well.
- Heat up a pan with the oil over medium high heat, add chicken, cook for 5 minutes and Add aminos, ketchup, vinegar, ginger, palm sugar and garlic, stir well, cover and cook on Low for 4 hours.
- Add cashews and green onion, stir, divide into bowls and serve.
- Enjoy!

Nutrition:

- Calories - 200
- Fat - 3
- Carbs - 8
- Protein - 12

CHICKEN RICE WITH LEMON

Preparation time: 20 minutes

Cooking time: 9 hours

Serving: 7

Ingredients:

- 16 oz chicken thighs
- 2 lemon
- 1 cup white rice
- 1 teaspoon salt
- 1 teaspoon turmeric
- 1 teaspoon ground black pepper

- 1 teaspoon cilantro
- 1 teaspoon oregano
- 1 teaspoon chili flakes
- 2 tablespoons butter
- 3 garlic cloves
- 7 oz tomatoes, canned
- 5 oz white onion
- ½ cup green peas, frozen
- 5 oz chicken stock
- 1 oz bay leaf

Directions:

- Peel the garlic cloves and slice them. Toss the butter in a saute pan and melt it. Sprinkle the melted butter with the salt, turmeric, ground black pepper, cilantro, oregano, chili flakes, sliced garlic, and bay leaf.
- Roast the mixture on the high heat for 30 seconds, stirring constantly. After this, place the chicken thighs in the pan and sear the chicken for 4 minutes on the both side.
- Meanwhile, pour the chicken stock in the slow cooker bowl. Add green peas, canned tomatoes, and white rice.
- Peel the white onion and slice it.
- Close the lid and cook the dish for 9 hours on LOW. When the dish is cooked, chill it gently.
- Enjoy!

Nutrition:

- Calories - 292
- Fat - 10.7
- Carbs - 34.78
- Protein - 16

WONDERFUL SALSA CHICKEN

Preparation time: 10 minutes

Cooking time: 7 hours

Serving: 4

Ingredients:

- 4 chicken breasts, skinless and boneless
- ½ cup water
- 16 ounces Paleo salsa
- 1 and ½ tablespoons parsley, dried
- 1 teaspoon garlic powder
- ½ tablespoon cilantro, chopped
- 1 teaspoon onion powder
- ½ tablespoons oregano, dried
- ½ teaspoon paprika, smoked

- 1 teaspoon chili powder
- ½ teaspoon cumin, ground
- Black pepper to the taste

Directions:

- Put the water in your slow cooker and add chicken breasts.
- Add salsa, parsley, garlic powder, cilantro, onion powder, oregano, paprika, chili powder, cumin and black pepper to the taste.
- Stir, cover and cook on Low for 7 hours.
- Divide chicken on plates, drizzle the sauces on top and serve.
- Enjoy!

Nutrition:

- Calories - 200
- Fat - 4
- Carbs - 7
- Protein - 9

CHICKEN TACOS WITH MANGO SALSA

Serving: 6

Ingredients:

- Cooking spray
- 2 large boneless and skinless chicken breasts
- 1 ½ cups mango salsa, plus some extra for garnishing
- 1 dollop of sour cream
- Mexican blend shredded cheese
- 12 small flour tortillas
- Lettuce (optional

Directions:

- Grease the slow cooker with cooking spray.
- Place the chicken and mango salsa in the slow cooker. Cover and cook for 4 ½ hours on LOW.
- Combine the cheese and sour cream. Mix well.
- Spread the cheese mixture on top of the chicken and allow to melt in the slow cooker for another 10-15 minutes.
- Serve in the tortillas with topping of your choice, if desired.

Nutrition:

- Calories - 375
- Fat - 8.4 g
- Carbs - 35.1 g
- Protein - 43.3 g

SPICY CHICKEN STEW

Preparation + Cooking time: 35 minutes

Serving: 4

Ingredients:

- 10 oz chicken breast, chopped into bite-sized pieces
- 4 tbsp olive oil
- 1 onion, finely chopped
- 1 cup cabbage, shredded
- 2 celery stalks, finely chopped
- 2 garlic cloves, whole
- 1 cup Greek yogurt, plain
- 4 cups chicken stock
- Spices: 1 tsp salt
- 1 tsp cumin powder
- ½ tsp coriander powder
- 1 tsp garlic powder
- 2 tbsp chili powder
- 1 tbsp cayenne pepper

Directions:

- Rinse the meat and place on a large cutting board. Cut into bite-sized pieces and place in a deep bowl.
- Season with spices coat well. Set aside.
- Plug in the instant pot and press the "Saute" button. Heat up the olive oil and add onions, garlic, and celery stalk.
- Stir well and cook for 5-6 minutes, stirring constantly.
- Now add the meat and continue to cook for 3-4 minutes.
- Finally, add shredded cabbage and stir well. Pour in the stock and seal the lid.
- Set the steam release handle to the "Sealing" position and press the "MANUAL" button.
- Set the timer for 13 minutes on high pressure.
- When done, release the pressure naturally for 10-15 minutes and then open the lid. Chill for a while and stir in Greek yogurt before serving.

Nutrition:

- Calories - 293
- Fat - 17.8g
- Carbs - 5.9g
- Protein - 26.9g

KETO SALSA CHICKEN

Preparation time: 10 minutes

Cooking time: 9 hours

Serving: 4

Ingredients:

- 3 oz Monterey Jack cheese, shredded
- 1-pound chicken breast, skinless, boneless
- 1/3 cup salsa
- 1 teaspoon almond butter

Directions:

- Put almond butter in the crockpot.
- Then place the chicken breast there and top it with salsa.
- After this, sprinkle the salsa with Monterey Jack cheese and close the lid.
- Cook salsa chicken on Low for 9 hours.

Nutrition:

- Calories - 239
- Fat - 11.6
- Carbs - 2.3
- Protein - 30.4

BRIE AND PANCETTA STUFFED TURKEY BREAST WITH BLACKBERRIES

Serving: 6

Ingredients:

- 1 cup pancetta, diced
- 1 ½ pounds turkey breast
- 1 tablespoon olive oil
- 1 teaspoon salt
- 1 teaspoon black pepper
- 1 cup Brie, sliced
- 1 tablespoon fresh thyme
- 2 cloves garlic, crushed and minced
- 1 cup blackberries
- 1 cup onions, sliced
- ½ cup chicken stock
- 1 tablespoon balsamic vinegar
- 1 sprig fresh rosemary

Directions:

- Cook the pancetta in a skillet over medium heat until it is lightly browned, approximately 3-4 minutes. Remove it from the heat and allow it to cool slightly.
- Cut a slit along the side of each turkey breast to create a pocket for the stuffing.
- Brush or drizzle both sides of the turkey with olive oil and season with salt and black pepper.

- In a bowl, combine the pancetta, Brie, thyme, and garlic. Mix well and then stuff the
- mixture into the center of the turkey breast. Secure with kitchen twine or wooden picks, and place the turkey breasts in the slow cooker.
- Add the blackberries and onions to the slow cooker, followed by the chicken stock, balsamic vinegar, and rosemary.
- Cover and cook on low for 8 hours.

Nutrition:

- Calories - 371.7
- Fat - 19.5 g
- Carbs - 5.6 g
- Protein - 41.4 g

ROAST CHICKEN

Serving: 6-8

Ingredients:

- 1 4-pound whole chicken, with the giblets, removed
- 3 stalks celery, cut into thirds
- 1 ½ cups vegetables of your choice (for example, carrot, leeks, squash, sweet potato or parsnip, cut into chunks
- 1 head garlic, halved
- 2 small onions, halved, divided
- 1 lemon, halved
- freshly ground black pepper and paprika, for sprinkling
- For the rub
- 2 teaspoons sea salt
- 1/2 teaspoon garlic powder
- 1 teaspoon dried thyme
- 1 teaspoon white pepper (optional)

Directions:

- Pat the chicken dry using paper towels.
- Combine the ingredients for the rub in a bowl.
- Lay the celery and carrot (or whatever veggies you're using) on the bottom of the slow cooker insert. This will help to hold the chicken while cooking and keep it from coming into contact with the bottom of the pot and drying out.
- Spread the rub evenly inside and outside the whole chicken.
- Stuff the chicken with the garlic, 2 slices of onion and lemon. If there's not enough space, remove some of the onion or garlic and add to the other vegetables outside
- the chicken.
- Sprinkle with paprika and spread evenly. This will give the chicken a more "roasted" look when cooked.
- Sprinkle with freshly ground black pepper.
- Lift the chicken into the pot, placing it over the vegetables with the breast-side up.
- Fold and tuck the wings under the chicken.

- Cook for 6 hours on LOW or 4 hours on HIGH. The cooking time will vary, depending on the size of the chicken. The internal temperature should reach 160ËšF.
- OPTIONAL: For a more oven-roasted look, carefully lift the chicken into an oven-safe dish and place in a hot broiler to brown (for about 5 minutes). Turn off the oven heat but leave the chicken in the broiler for 5 to 10 minutes longer.
- Strain out the broth and keep for future recipes.

Nutrition:

- Calories - 463
- Fat - 12.3 g
- Carbs - 0.2 g
- Protein - 82.1 g

BEEF, PORK AND LAMB

SPIRAL HAM

Preparation time: 10 minutes

Cooking time: 4.5 hours

Serving: 7

Ingredients:

- 1-pound spiral ham
- 2 tablespoons Erythritol
- 3 tablespoons butter
- 4 tablespoons lemon juice

Directions:

- Put Erythritol and butter in the pan and preheat it until butter is melted.
- Add lemon juice and simmer the liquid for 1 minute.
- Then place the spiral ham in the crockpot.
- Pour the sweet lemon liquid over the ham and close the lid.
- Cook the spiral ham on High for 4.5 hours.

Nutrition:

- Calories - 174
- Fat - 11.8
- Carbs - 7.5
- Protein - 13.2

LAMB SHOULDER HASH

Preparation + Cooking time: 35 minutes

Serving: 3

Ingredients:

- 9 oz lamb shoulder, chopped into bite-sized pieces
- 1 large tomato, finely chopped
- 2 green bell peppers, finely chopped
- 2 celery stalks, finely chopped
- ¼ cup almonds, minced
- 3 large eggs
- 2 tbsp olive oil
- 2 tbsp butter
- ¼ cup beef broth
- Spices: 1 tsp salt
- ½ tsp garlic powder
- ¼ tsp black pepper, ground

Directions:

- Plug in the instant pot and grease the inner pot with oil. Add chopped meat and season with salt.
- Cook for 5-6 minutes and then add bell peppers and celery stalks.
- Continue to cook for 10 minutes, stirring occasionally.
- Now pour in the stock and add tomatoes. Bring it to a boil and simmer for 15 minutes.
- When most of the liquid has evaporated, stir in the butter and season with garlic powder and black pepper.
- Optionally, add some more salt.
- Gently crack the eggs and continue to cook until completely set.

Nutrition:

- Calories - 465
- Fat - 32.6g
- Carbs - 7.9g
- Protein - 33.7g

GROUND PORK BURGERS

Preparation + Cooking time: 15 minutes

Serving: 6

Ingredients:

- 1-pound ground pork
- 2 onions
- 3 tablespoon almond flour
- 1/2 cup fresh parsley; finely chopped
- 1 red chili pepper
- 1/4 teaspoon black pepper; freshly ground.
- 1/4 teaspoon garlic powder

- 1/2 teaspoon salt

Directions:

- Place the onions and chili pepper in a food processor and process for 30 seconds. Mix well and shape burgers, about 2-inch in diameter.
- Place burgers in the steam basket and pour in one cup of water in the inner pot.
- Seal the lid and set the steam release handle to the "SEALING" position. Press the "MANUAL" button and set the timer for 7 minutes on high pressure
- When done, perform a quick pressure release and open the lid. Remove burgers from the pot and serve immediately.

Nutrition:

- Calories - 198
- Fat - 4.9g
- Carbs - 4.4g
- Protein - 30.9g

LAMB CURRY

Preparation + Cooking time: 1 hour 30 minutes

Serving: 4-6

Ingredients:

- 1½ lbs lamb stew meat, cubed
- ½ cup coconut milk
- 4 cloves garlic, minced
- Juice of ½ lime
- 1-inch piece fresh ginger, grated
- ¼ tsp sea salt
- ¼ tsp ground black pepper
- 1½ tbsp yellow curry powder
- ½ tsp turmeric
- 1 tbsp butter
- 14 oz can tomatoes, diced
- 3 medium carrots, sliced
- 1 medium onion, diced
- 1 medium zucchini, diced
- Cilantro, chopped

Directions:

- In the Instant Pot, combine the milk, garlic, lime juice, ginger, salt and pepper. Mix well.
- Add the lamb cubes to the pot and stir well until fully coated.
- Let marinate for at least 45 minutes.
- Add the curry powder, turmeric, butter, tomatoes, carrots, and onion.
- Close and lock the lid. Select MANUAL and cook at HIGH pressure for 22 minutes.
- When the timer beeps, let the pressure

- Release Naturally
- for 10 minutes, then release any remaining steam manually. Open the lid.
- Add the zucchini. Select SAUTE and simmer the dish for 6-8 minutes until the zucchini is tender.
- Top with cilantro and serve.

SPRING PORK STEW

Preparation time: 10 minutes

Cooking time: 4.5 hours

Serving: 5

Ingredients:

- ¼ cup fresh parsley, chopped
- 1 tablespoon fresh dill, chopped
- 1 tablespoon chives, chopped
- 1/3 cup kale, chopped
- 1 zucchini, chopped
- 1 cup of water
- ½ cup of coconut milk
- ½ teaspoon thyme
- ½ teaspoon ground coriander
- 1 teaspoon salt
- 1 teaspoon coconut oil
- 1 teaspoon chili powder
- ½ teaspoon cayenne pepper
- 1-pound pork chops, chopped

Directions:

- In the shallow bowl, mix up together cayenne pepper, chili powder, ground coriander, and thyme.
- Then place the pork chops in the crockpot.
- Add coconut oil, salt, and spice mixture.
- After this, add coconut milk, water, zucchini, chives, and fresh parsley.
- Mix up the ingredients gently and cook for 4 hours on High.
- Then use the spatula to combine all ingredients again and add kale and dill.
- Close the lid and cook the stew for 30 minutes on High.

Nutrition:

- Calories - 367
- Fat - 29.4
- Carbs - 4.1
- Protein - 21.9

SLOW COOKED BEEF AND BAKED BEANS

Serving: 4

Ingredients:

- 1 pound ground beef
- 1 large onion, diced
- 15 ounces baked beans
- 1 14 ounce can diced tomatoes with green chilies (undrained
- In a medium skillet, heat the oil and brown the beef, together with the onion, green pepper, celery, and garlic.
- Cover, and cook for 8-9 hours on LOW.
- 1 can of spicy vegetable juice
- Optional: cheddar cheese or sour cream, for garnishing

Directions:

- Cook the meat and onion until browned, and drain the excess fat.
- Put the mixture in the slow cooker.
- In a bowl, mix the beans, tomatoes and chilies, and vegetable juice.
- Pour over meat and mix well.
- Cover and cook for 4-6 hour on LOW.
- Plate and serve garnished with cream cheese or sour cream

Nutrition:

- Calories - 332
- Fat - 12 g
- Carbs - 31 g
- Protein - 23 g

PORK CUTLETS WITH BUTTON MUSHROOMS

Preparation + Cooking time: 25 minutes

Serving: 4

Ingredients:

- 2 pork cutlets; boneless
- 2 cups button mushrooms; sliced
- 1 cup shiitake mushrooms; sliced
- 1 onion; finely chopped
- 1/2 cup heavy cream
- 2 garlic cloves; crushed
- 2 tablespoon fresh parsley; finely chopped.
- 4 tablespoon oil
- 1 teaspoon dried thyme
- 1/2 teaspoon black pepper; freshly ground.
- 1 teaspoon salt

Directions:

- Rinse the meat and pat dry with a kitchen paper. Using a sharp knife, carefully chop the meat into bite-sized pieces. Season with salt and pepper, Set aside.
- Plug in the instant pot and press the "SAUTE" button. Grease the inner pot with oil and add onions and garlic. Saute for 3-4 mintues and then add mushrooms. Pour in the heavy cream and cook for 2-3 minutes
- Now add the meat and season with thyme. Give it a good stir and pour in 1/4 cup of water.
- Cook for 12-15 minutes, stirring occasionally. Stir in the parsley and press the "CANCEL" button.
- Optionally sprinkle with some grated Parmesan cheese before serving

Nutrition:

- Calories - 356
- Fat - 22.9g
- Carbs - 8g
- Protein - 28.6g

GARLIC PORK RECIPE

Preparation + Cooking time: 45 minutes

Serving: 6

Ingredients:

- 2 -pounds pork chops
- 1 cup cherry tomatoes
- 1/4 cup soy sauce
- 2 large onions; finely chopped
- 4 garlic cloves
- 3 tablespoon butter
- 1/2 cup celery stalks; chopped
- 3 tablespoon apple cider vinegar
- 1/2 teaspoon ginger powder
- 2 tablespoon stevia crystal
- 1/2 teaspoon chili flakes
- 1 teaspoon salt

Directions:

- Rinse well the meat and pat dry each piece with some kitchen paper. Place on a large cutting board and remove the bones. Chop into bite-sized pieces and place in a deep bowl. Sprinkle with salt, ginger, and chili flakes. Drizzle with soy sauce and set aside.
- Plug in the instant pot and press the "SAUTE" button. Grease the inner pot with butter and heat up. Add onions, garlic, and celery stalks. Cook for 3-4 minutes, stirring constantly. Now add cherry tomatoes and sprinkle with stevia. Continue to cook for 5 minutes or until soft.
- Finally, add the meat and drizzle with apple cider vinegar. Stir fry for another 4-5 minutes and then pour in one cup of water.

- Press the "CANCEL" button and seal the lid. Set the steam release handle to the "SEALING" position and press the "MANUAL" button
- Set the timer for 10 minutes on high pressure. When done, release the pressure naturally and open the lid. Optionally, sprinkle with freshly chopped parsley and serve immediately.

Nutrition:

- Calories - 569
- Fat - 43.5g
- Carbs - 5.3g
- Protein - 35.6g

TURMERIC MEATLOAF SLICES

Preparation time: 15 minutes

Cooking time: 4.5 hours

Serving: 4

Ingredients:

- 1 teaspoon ground turmeric
- 1 teaspoon ground paprika
- 1 teaspoon onion powder
- ½ teaspoon salt
- 1 teaspoon chili powder
- 1 ½ cup ground pork
- 2 eggs, beaten
- Cooking spray

Directions:

- Spray the loaf mold with cooking spray.
- In the separated bowl mix up together ground turmeric, ground paprika, onion powder, salt, chili powder, ground pork, and eggs.
- When the meat mixture is homogenous, Arrange the mold in the crockpot and close the lid.
- Cook the meatloaf for 4.5 hours on High.
- Then remove it from the crockpot and chill well.
- Remove the meatloaf from the mold and slice it.

Nutrition:

- Calories - 273
- Fat - 18.8
- Carbs - 1.7
- Protein - 23.1

COFFEE ROAST BEEF RECIPE

Serving: 12

Ingredients:

- Meat Rub: 5 cloves garlic, minced
- 1½ teaspoons salt
- ¾ teaspoons pepper, ground
- Beef: 3½ - 4 pounds boneless beef chuck roast
- ¾ cup brewed coffee, strong
- Sauce: 2 tablespoons cornstarch
- ¼ cup water, cold

Directions:

- Mix together the meat rub ingredients, then rub it all over the beef.
- Place the seasoned meat into the crock pot and cover with coffee.
- Cook everything on LOW for 8 to 10 hours.
- Bring the liquid to a boil.
- Mix the corn starch and water together, then slowly pour into the boiling liquid. Cook for 1 to 2 minutes.
- Pour the sauce over the meat and serve.

Nutrition:

- Calories - 199
- Fat - 11 g
- Carbs - 2 g
- Protein - 22 g

CORNED BEEF (PRESSURE COOKED

Serving: 4

Ingredients:

- 2-pound packet of corned beef brisket with seasoning
- 4 red potatoes, cut into chunks
- 1 pound baby carrots, chopped and peeled
- 1 head of cabbage, sliced
- 2 cloves garlic, minced
- 2 tablespoons sugar
- 2 tablespoons apple cider vinegar
- Salt and black pepper, to taste

Directions:

- Place the potatoes, cabbage, and carrots into the Crock-Pot
-
- Express.
- Add the garlic, sugar, apple cider vinegar, salt, and black pepper on top of the vegetables.

- Rub the packet seasoning on the beef and place it inside the pot.
- Secure the lid of the Crock-Pot Express.
- Press the MEAT/STEW button and set the timer for 30 minutes at high pressure.

Nutrition:

- Calories - 645
- Fat - 29 g
- Carbs - 60 g
- Protein - 37.5 g

SMOKY BABY BACK RIBS

Serving: 4

Ingredients:

- 2 baby back pork ribs racks, halved
- 1 cup barbecue sauce
- 1 teaspoon of liquid smoke (optional
- 4 tablespoons barbecue spices mix
- Cooking spray

Directions:

- Remove the membrane and excess fat from the ribs.
- Rub each rib half rack with 1 tablespoon of the barbecue spice mix.
- Spray slow cooker with cooking spray.
- Place pork ribs in slow cooker.
- Combine the barbecue sauce and liquid smoke. Brush the racks lightly with half of the liquid smoke and barbecue sauce mix.
- Cook on HIGH for 5 hours until tender.
- When ready to serve, remove ribs from slow cooker, and place them on a foil lined baking dish. Brush ribs with remaining barbecue sauce.
- Broil the ribs in the oven for about 5-10 minutes. Watch carefully so they don't burn. This can also be done on the barbecue grill.
- Serve warm with your favorite side dishes.

Nutrition:

- Calories - 682
- Fat - 43 g
- Carbs - 21 g
- Protein - 56 g

BEEF AND MUSHROOM RECIPE

Serving: 6

Ingredients:

- 2 tablespoons vegetable oil
- 1 pound cremini mushroom, sliced
- 1 white onion, sliced
- 2 pounds beef sirloin steak, cut into bite-size slices
- Salt and pepper, to taste
- 4 cloves garlic, minced
- 1 tablespoon paprika
- ½ cup tomato paste
- 2 cups low-sodium beef broth
- 1 teaspoon all-purpose flour
- 2 tablespoons Worcestershire sauce
- 1 cup parsley, chopped fresh
- 14 ounces egg noodles, cooked

Directions:

- Press the BROWN/SAUTe button on the pot and set the temperature to high.
- Press the START/STOP button.
- Allow the pot to preheat.
- Add the oil along with the onions, mushrooms, and beef.
- Cook for 5 minutes.
- Add salt, pepper and tomato paste.
- Cook for one minute.
- Add garlic and paprika, broth, and Worcestershire sauce.
- Take some liquid from the pot and mix it with the flour.
- Add the flour mixture to the pot.
- Press the START/STOP button.
- Secure the lid and select slow cook at low temperature for 4 hours.
- Press START/STOP and let cook for 4 hours.
- Serve the cooked mixture over egg noodles.
- Enjoy with a garnish of parsley.

Nutrition:

- Calories - 360
- Fat - 7 g
- Carbs - 30 g
- Protein - 43 g

BEEF STROGANOFF

Preparation + Cooking time: 20 minutes

Serving: 4

Ingredients:

- 1 small Onion (diced)
- 2 cloves Garlic (crushed)
- 2 rashers Bacon (diced)
- 1 lbs. Beef Sirloin Steak (cut into ½ inch strips)

- 1 tsp Smoked Paprika
- 3 tbsp. tomato paste
- 1 cup Beef Broth
- ½ lbs. Mushrooms (quartered)
- ½ cup Sour Cream

Directions:

- Place all ingredients, except sour cream, in the Instant Pot and stir to combine.
- Place and lock the lid and manually set the cooking time to 20 minutes at high pressure.
- Let naturally release the pressure and then stir in the sour cream.
- Serve warm.

Nutrition:

- Calories - 260
- Fat - 14g
- Carbs - 4.8g
- Protein - 26.5g

MEDITERRANEAN RICE AND SAUSAGE

Serving: 6

Ingredients:

- 1½ pounds Italian sausage, crumbled
- 1 medium onion, chopped
- 2 tablespoons steak sauce
- 2 cups long grain rice, uncooked
- 1 (14-ounce can diced tomatoes with juice
- ½ cup water
- 1 medium green pepper, diced

Directions:

- Spray your slow cooker with olive oil or nonstick cooking spray.
- Add the sausage, onion, and steak sauce to the slow cooker.
- Cook on low for 8 to 10 hours.
- After 8 hours, add the rice, tomatoes, water and green pepper. Stir to combine thoroughly.
- Cook an additional 20 to 25 minutes or until the rice is cooked.

Nutrition:

- Calories - 650
- Fat - 36 g
- Carbs - 57 g
- Protein - 22 g

EASY LAMB HOTPOT

Serving: 2

Preparation time: 10 minutes

Cooking time: 4 hours

Ingredients:

- 1 cup lamb stock
- 2/3 lb diced lamb leg
- 1 1/2 large potatoes in 3mm slices
- 1 large carrot in bitesize pieces

Directions:

- In a crock-pot, add a little oil plus the onion and carrot. Cover and cook on a low for 5 minutes or until soft but not brown.
- Change to high then add lamb. Cook for 2-3 minutes until browned.
- Add the lamb stock and a little salt and pepper.
- Arrange the potato slices for them to slightly overlap.
- Cover and cook for 4 hours on high.

Nutrition:

- Calories - 310
- Fat - 8g
- Carbs - 7g
- Protein - 36g
- Cholesterol - 97mg
- Sodium - 306mg
- Serving suggestions: Serve just as it is or with extra vegetables.

PORK AND VEGETABLES WITH NOODLES

Preparation + Cooking time: 20 minutes

Serving: 6

Ingredients:

- 1-pound ground pork
- 1 tablespoon oil
- 4 cups baby spinach; chopped.
- 1/2 cup parmesan cheese; grated
- 1/2 cup onion; chopped.
- 2 garlic
- 1 cup bell peppers; chopped
- 2 packages shirataki noodles; cooked

Directions:

- Turn your Instant Pot to "SAUTE" ,* and when it's hot, add oil. Once the oil is hot, add ground pork.
- Saute until meat is crumbled and pork is only slightly pink
- Add onions, peppers, spinach, and garlic, and mix well
- Cook on high pressure for 3 minutes. When time is up, release pressure quickly
- Pour sauce over shirataki noodles, and sprinkle all of it with the shredded cheese.

Nutrition:

- Calories - 241
- Carbs - 5 g
- Carbs - 2.3 g
- Fat - 18 g
- Protein - 15g

BRISKET DELIGHT RECIPE

Serving: 6

Ingredients:

- 1 boneless beef chuck roast (3 pounds, halved
- 1 envelope chili seasoning
- ½ cup barbecue sauce
- 8 onion slices (optional)
- 8 slices cheddar cheese (optional)
- 8 hamburger buns (optional)

Directions:

- Place the beef chuck halves in a slow cooker and sprinkle the chili seasoning on top.
- Pour the barbecue sauce over the seasoned chuck.
- Cook on LOW for 8 to 10 hours, then remove the beef from heat.
- Shred the meat and remove the fat from the liquid in the slow cooker.
- Place the meat back into the sauce and let sit for 10 minutes.
- Place the meat on top of the hamburger buns, and top with onions and cheese.

Nutrition:

- Calories - 262
- Fat - 6 g
- Carbs - 21 g
- Protein - 30 g

TENDER RACK OF LAMB

Preparation time: 15 minutes

Cooking time: 8 hours

Serving: 4

Ingredients:

- 1 tablespoon mayonnaise
- 1 tablespoon canola oil
- ¼ teaspoon chili powder
- ½ teaspoon cayenne pepper
- ½ teaspoon salt
- 1-pound rack of lamb
- ½ cup fresh spinach
- ¼ cup of water

Directions:

- Put the fresh spinach in the blender and blend it until smooth.
- Then add mayonnaise, canola oil, chili powder, cayenne pepper, and salt.
- Blend the mixture for 10 seconds.
- After this, pour water in the crockpot.
- Rub the rack of lamb with spinach mixture generously.
- Arrange the meat in the crockpot and add remaining spinach blend.
- Close the lid.
- Cook the rack of lamb for 8 hours on Low.

Nutrition:

- Calories - 238
- Fat - 14.9
- Carbs - 1.2
- Protein - 23.3

KOREAN SHORT RIBS

Serving: 10

Preparation time: 5 minutes

Cooking time: 45 minutes

Ingredients:

- 5 pounds short ribs
- ½ cup coconut aminos
- 1 tablespoon rice vinegar
- 2 teaspoons fish sauce
- 1 medium pear, peeled and grated
- 6 cloves of garlic, minced
- 1 onion, chopped
- 1 thumb-size ginger, grated

Directions:

- Place all ingredients in the Instant Pot except for the feta cheese.

- Close the lid and press the Meat/Stew button.
- Adjust the cooking time to 45 minutes.
- Do natural pressure release.

Nutrition:

- Calories - 363
- Carbs - 40.6g
- Protein - 21.1g
- Fat - 12.9g

MEXICAN SHREDDED BEEF

Serving: 2

Preparation time: 15 minutes

Cooking time: 5 hours

Ingredients:

- 1/3 tsp ground cu minutes
- 1/3 tbsp chili powder
- 1 chuck roast
- 1/8 cup bacon fat or lard
- 1 can diced tomatoes

Directions:

- Rub the roast with salt and pepper to taste.
- Add all ingredients in a crock-pot. Add a few tablespoons of water and some garlic to taste.
- Cover and cook for 5 hours on low.

Nutrition:

- Calories - 416
- Fat - 27.82g
- Carbs - 1.4g
- Protein - 29.51g

INDIAN PORK

Preparation time: 14 minutes

Cooking time: 5 hours

Serving: 8

Ingredients:

- 21 oz pork steak, tenderized
- 2 tablespoon curry
- 1 teaspoon harissa
- 1 tablespoon garam masala
- 1 teaspoon chili flakes
- ½ cup cream
- 1 teaspoon ground black pepper
- 1 teaspoon salt
- 1 teaspoon sugar
- 1 cup cashew, crushed
- 1 teaspoon ground nutmeg

Directions:

- Rub the pork steaks with the curry, harissa, garam masala, and chili flakes.
- Sprinkle the meat with the salt and sugar. Then combine the cream with the ground black pepper and ground nutmeg.
- Whisk the cream mix and pour it into the slow cooker.
- Add the pork steaks and close the lid. Cook the dish on HIGH for 5 hours.
- Then Serve it!

Nutrition:

- Calories - 434
- Fat - 33.4
- Carbs - 12.27
- Protein - 23

SWEET COCONUT PORK

Preparation + Cooking time: 1 hour

Serving: 6

Ingredients:

- 4 pork chops, with bones
- 1 large onion, finely chopped
- 1 chili pepper, finely chopped
- 1 cup heavy cream
- ¼ cup coconut milk
- 2 tbsp coconut cream
- 3 tbsp almond flour
- 2 tbsp butter
- 1 cup cauliflower, chopped into florets

Spices:

- 1 tsp salt
- ½ tsp white pepper, freshly ground
- 2 tsp stevia powder

- 1 tsp rum extract

Directions:

- In a medium-sized bowl, combine heavy cream, coconut milk, coconut cream, salt, pepper, stevia, and rum. Add the meat and coat well with the mixture. Seal the bag and refrigerate overnight.
- Plug in the instant pot and set the trivet at the bottom of the inner pot. Remove the pork from the refrigerator and place in a deep oven-safe bowl along with the marinade.
- Place the bowl in the pot and pour in about one cup of water in the inner pot. Seal the lid and set the steam release handle to the "Sealing" posisiton.
- Press the "MANUAL" button and set the timer for 20 minutes on high pressure.
- When done, perform a quick pressure release and open the lid. Remove the bowl with the pork and press the "Saute" button.
- Grease the inner pot with butter and heat up. Add onions, peppers, and cauliflower.
- Stir well and cook for 6-7 minutes.
- Now add the pork along with its sauce and stir in almond flour. Continue to cook for another 3-4 minutes, coating the meat well with the sauce.
- Press the "Cancel" button and serve immediately.

Nutrition:

- Calories - 462
- Fat - 24.6g
- Carbs - 7.9g
- Protein - 49.4g

SOUR AND SWEET MEATBALLS

Serving: 2

Ingredients:

- 16 pork meatballs, pre-cooked
- ½ cup sugar
- 2 tablespoons cornstarch
- ½ cup white vinegar
- 1 tablespoon soy sauce
- ½ teaspoon chili garlic sauce
- 1 teaspoon sesame oil
- ½ green pepper, diced
- 1 can pineapple chunks
- Cooked rice, for serving

Directions:

- Place the meatballs in a slow cooker.
- In a mixing bowl, whisk together the sugar, cornstarch, vinegar, soy sauce, chili garlic sauce, and sesame oil. Mix all together and pour over the meatballs.
- Add the green pepper.
- Cover, and cook for 4-4 ½ hours on LOW.

- Add the pineapple and cook for 30 minutes more.
- Serve over hot rice.

Nutrition:

- Calories - 794
- Fat - 29 g
- Carbs - 94 g
- Protein - 39 g

KETO PORK FILLETS

Preparation + Cooking time: 30 minutes

Serving: 4

Ingredients:

- 1-pound pork fillet; central cut
- 1 green bell pepper; finely chopped.
- 1 small chili pepper
- 2 tablespoon balsamic vinegar
- 1 pickle; sliced
- 2 boiled eggs
- 1/4 cup fresh parsley; finely chopped
- 3 tablespoon butter
- 2 small onions; finely chopped.
- 3 bacon slices; chopped.
- 2-ounce prosciutto
- 1 teaspoon smoked pepper

Directions:

- Plug in the instant pot and press the "SAUTE" button. Heat the butter and add onions, bacon, prosciutto, bell pepper, and chili pepper
- Cook for 3-4 minutes, stirring constantly and then add pickle and season with smoked pepper. Drizzle with balsamic vinegar and continue to cook for one minute.
- Now add the fillets and pour in 1/2 cup of water. Simmer for 10-15 minutes, turning a couple of times.
- When done; press the "CANCEL" button.

Nutrition:

- Calories - 396
- Fat - 21.7g
- Carbs - 5.4g
- Protein - 41.7g

SAUCY MUSHROOM PORK

Serving: 8

87

Ingredients:

- 2 pounds pork tenderloin medallions
- 1 teaspoon salt
- 1 teaspoon black pepper
- 1 teaspoon paprika
- 2 tablespoons butter
- 1 cup onion, sliced
- 3 cups mushrooms, quartered
- 4 cloves garlic, crushed and minced
- 2 teaspoons rubbed sage
- 1 cup chicken stock
- 3 cups fresh spinach, chopped
- 1 cup heavy cream
- ½ cup cream cheese, cubed

Directions:

- Season the tenderloin medallions with salt, black pepper, and paprika, and place them in the slow cooker.
- Melt the butter in a skillet over medium heat.
- Saute the onion for 4-5 minutes, and add it to the slow cooker.
- Next, add the mushrooms, garlic, and rubbed sage. Toss gently to mix.
- Add the chicken stock.
- Cover and cook on low for 8 hours.
- Remove the lid and add the spinach, heavy cream, and cream cheese. Mix well, cover and cook an additional 15-20 minutes before serving.

Nutrition:

- Calories - 423
- Fat - 28.5 g
- Carbs - 4.5 g
- Protein - 36.5 g

SNACKS

DECADENT LIVER PATE

Preparation + Cooking time: 25 minutes

Serving: 6

Ingredients:

- 1 tsp olive oil
- 1 roughly chopped medium yellow onion
- Salt and freshly ground black pepper, to taste
- ¾ pound grass-fed chicken livers
- 1 bay leaf

- ¼ cup homemade chicken broth
- 1 tbsp. fresh lemon juice
- 2 anchovies in oil
- 1 tbsp. capers
- 1 tbsp. butter

Directions:

- Place the oil in the Instant Pot and select "Saute". Then add the onion with a little salt and black pepper and cook for about 2-3 minutes.
- Add the chicken livers and bay leaf and cook for about 2 minutes.
- Add the broth and scrape brown bits from the bottom.
- Select the "Cancel" and stir the mixture once.
- Secure the lid and place the pressure valve to "Seal" position.
- Select "MANUAL" and cook under "High Pressure" for about 5 minutes.
- Select the "Cancel" and carefully do a Natural release.
- Remove the lid and discard the bay leaf.
- Stir in anchovies and capers and with a stick blender, blend the mixture until pureed.
- Stir in butter and rum and Refrigerate to chill before serving.

Nutrition:

- Calories - 142
- Fat - 7.3g
- Carbs - 0.4g
- Protein - 15.7g

ROSEMARY FINGERLING POTATOES

Preparation time: 16 minutes

Cooking time: 8 hours

Serving: 15

Ingredients:

- 2 lb. fingerling potatoes
- 8 oz bacon
- 1 teaspoon onion powder
- 1 teaspoon chili powder
- 1 teaspoon garlic powder
- 1 teaspoon paprika
- 3 tablespoons butter
- 1 teaspoon dried dill
- 1 tablespoon rosemary

Directions:

- Wash the fingerling potatoes carefully.
- Butter the slow cooker bowl and make a layer of fingerling potatoes there.

- Combine the onion powder, chili powder, garlic powder, paprika, and dried dill together in a separate bowl.
- Stir lightly. Sprinkle the layer of fingerling potatoes with the spice mixture.
- Then slice the bacon and combine it with the rosemary.
- Cover the fingerling potatoes with the sliced bacon and close the slow cooker lid. Cook the dish on LOW for 8 hours. Serve the snack immediately. Enjoy!

Nutrition:

- Calories - 117
- Fat - 6.9
- Carbs - 12.07
- Protein - 3

OREGANO CHEESE DIP

Preparation time: 5 minutes

Cooking time: 2 hours

Serving: 4

Ingredients:

- ½ cup Cheddar cheese, shredded
- 2 oz Monterey Jack cheese, shredded
- 1 tablespoon dried oregano
- 2 tablespoon butter
- 1 teaspoon smoked paprika
- 2 oz Swiss cheese, grated
- ¼ cup coconut cream

Directions:

- Put all ingredients from the list above in the crockpot.
- Close the lid and cook the dip of High for 2 hours.

Nutrition:

- Calories - 254
- Fat - 22.4
- Carbs - 2.9
- Protein - 11.4

STUFFED MUSHROOMS

Preparation time: 10 minutes

Cooking time: 4 minutes

Serving: 4

Ingredients:

- 1 pound white mushrooms, stems removed
- 2 tablespoons olive oil
- 2 garlic cloves, minced
- 1/2 cup Italian seasoned breadcrumbs
- 1 cup shredded mozzarella cheese
- 1 cup water

Directions:

- Mix together oil, garlic, breadcrumbs, and cheese. Stuff the mushrooms with the breadcrumb mixture.
- Pour 1 cup water into the Instant Pot. Place the steamer basket over the water and arrange the mushrooms in the basket.
- Close lid and set cooking time for 4 minutes.

Nutrition:

- Calories - 231
- Fat - 14.26 g
- Carbs - 16.83 g
- Protein - 10.57 g

PORK LETTUCE FOLDS

Preparation time: 15 minutes

Cooking time: 4 hours

Serving: 4

Ingredients:

- 1 cup ground pork
- 1 teaspoon tomato paste
- 1 teaspoon chili flakes
- ¼ white onion, diced
- 8 lettuce leaves
- ¼ cup heavy cream
- 1 teaspoon coconut oil
- ½ teaspoon salt

Directions:

- Put the ground pork, tomato paste, chili flakes, onion, coconut oil, and salt in the crockpot.
- Add heavy cream and mix up the mixture very carefully.
- Close the lid and cook ground pork for 4 hours on High.
- Then mix up the cooked ground pork very carefully and chill for 10-15 minutes.
- Place 2 lettuce leaves to get the cross.

- Put the small amount of ground pork in the center of lettuce cross and fold it.
- Repeat the same steps with remaining lettuce leaves.

Nutrition:

- Calories - 273
- Fat - 20.2
- Carbs - 1.4
- Protein - 20.5

BBQ BISON PHYLLO BITES

Serving: 2

Preparation time: 15 minutes

Cooking time: 12 hours

Ingredients:

- 1 lb bison brisket
- 2 1/2 tsp Worcestershire sauce
- 1 3/4 tsp barbecue sauce
- 6 oz miniature phyllo dough shells
- 1 tbsp cheddar cheese, shredded

Directions:

- Except for the dough shells, combine all ingredients in the crockpot. Season with salt and pepper, 1 tsp vinegar, 1 clove of garlic and spices of choice.
- Add 1/4 cup of water.
- Cover and cook for 12 hours on low.
- Arrange phyllo doughs on a baking pan and divide the bison among them.
- Bake for 10 minutes at 375 F.

Nutrition:

- Calories - 119
- Fat - 3.5 g
- Carbs - 5.6 g
- Protein - 13.9 g
- Serving suggestions: Top with sour cream and fresh cilantro.

CHICKEN WINGS

Preparation time: 10 minutes

Cooking time: 4 hours

Serving: 4

Ingredients:

- ¼ cup coconut aminos
- ¼ cup balsamic vinegar
- 2 garlic cloves, minced
- 2 tablespoon stevia
- 1 teaspoon sriracha sauce
- 3 tablespoons lime juice
- Zest from 1 lime, grated
- 1 teaspoon ginger powder
- 2 teaspoons sesame seeds
- 2 pounds chicken wings
- 2 tablespoons chives, chopped

Directions:

- In your slow cooker, mix aminos with vinegar, garlic, stevia, sriracha, lime juice, lime zest and ginger and stir well.
- Add chicken wings, toss well, cover and cook on High for 4 hours.
- Arrange chicken wings on a platter, sprinkle chives and sesame seeds on top and serve as a casual appetizer.
- Enjoy!

Nutrition:

- Calories - 212
- Fat - 3
- Carbs - 12
- Protein - 3

VEGGIE SALSA

Preparation time: 10 minutes

Directions:

- In a bowl, mix coconut sugar with cinnamon and stir.
- In another bowl, mix egg white with vanilla and whisk well.
- Grease your slow cooker with cooking spray and add pecans.
- Add egg white mix and toss.
- Add coconut sugar mix, toss again, cover and cook on Low for 3 hours.
- Divide pecans into bowls and serve as a snack.
- Enjoy!

Nutrition:

- Calories - 172
- Fat - 3
- Carbs - 8
- Protein - 2

CHOCOLATE NUTS

Preparation time: 10 minutes

Cooking time: 2 hours 10 minutes

Serving: 4

Ingredients:

- 5 oz dark chocolate
- 5 oz milk chocolate
- 1 cup walnuts halves
- 2 teaspoons tablespoon heavy cream
- ¼ teaspoon vanilla extract

Directions:

- Chop the dark chocolate and milk chocolate and place them in the slow cooker.
- Add heavy cream and vanilla extract. Close the slow cooker lid and cook the chocolate on HIGH for 1 hours or till the mixture is homogenous.
- Then add the walnuts halves and stir.
- Cook the dish for 10 minutes on HIGH.
- Cover the tray with the parchment and Enjoy!

Nutrition:

- Calories - 521
- Fat - 35.1
- Carbs - 45.16
- Protein - 8

PECAN SNACK

Preparation time: 15 minutes

Cooking time: 3 hours

Serving: 7

Ingredients:

- 1 cup pecan
- 3 tablespoons flour
- 1 egg white
- 1 tablespoon sugar
- 1 tablespoon maple syrup

Directions:

- Whisk the egg white until you get stiff peaks.

- After this, add sugar and the maple syrup and whisk well.
- Then toss the pecans in the whisked egg white mixture and coat them well. Sprinkle the pecans with the flour and Cook the snack on HIGH for 3 hours. Stir the pecans every 30 minutes. When the dish is cooked, let it chill well. Serve it.

Nutrition:

- Calories - 124
- Fat - 10.2
- Carbs - 7.6
- Protein - 2

ZUCCHINI SPREAD

Preparation time: 5 minutes

Cooking time: 2 hours

Serving: 6

Ingredients:

- 2 pounds zucchini, chopped
- 1 tablespoon sesame paste
- 3 tablespoons lemon juice
- 1 garlic clove, minced
- ½ teaspoon coconut oil, melted

Directions:

- In your slow cooker, combine all the ingredients except the sesame paste. Cover and cook on low for 2 hours.
- Add the sesame paste and blend using an immersion blender. Divide into bowls and serve.

Nutrition:

- Calories - 46
- Fat - 2,1
- Carbs - 6
- Protein - 2,4

SOUR AND SWEET CHICKEN SLICES

Preparation time: 10 minutes

Cooking time: 4 hours

Serving: 2

Ingredients:

- 8 oz chicken fillets
- 1 teaspoon lemon juice
- ½ teaspoon Erythritol
- ½ teaspoon ground black pepper
- ¾ cup of water
- ¾ cup organic almond milk
- 1 teaspoon butter

Directions:

- Cut the chicken fillet into the slices and sprinkle them with lemon juice, Erythritol, ground black pepper, and water.
- Mix up the chicken slices well and Add butter and almond milk.
- Close the lid and cook chicken slices for 4 hours on High.

Nutrition:

- Calories - 264
- Fat - 11.6
- Carbs - 5.6
- Protein - 33.4

SOY SAUCE TOFU

Preparation time: 10 minutes

Cooking time: 2 ½ hour

Serving: 2

Ingredients:

- 1/2 tablespoon apple cider vinegar
- 1 tablespoon soy sauce
- 1/4 teaspoon garlic powder
- 1/4 teaspoon salt
- 1 container extra firm tofu, prepare 1-inch cubes
- 1/2 tablespoon red pepper flakes
- 3/4 cup ketchup
- 1 1/2 tablespoon brown sugar

Directions:

- Take Instant Pot and carefully arrange it over a clean, dry kitchen platform. Turn on the appliance.
- In the cooking pot area, add the mentioned ingredients. Stir the ingredients gently.
- Close the pot lid and seal the valve to avoid any leakage. Find and press "Slow cook" cooking setting and set cooking time to 2 hours 30 minutes.
- Allow the recipe ingredients to cook for the set time, and after that, the timer reads "zero".

- Press "Cancel" and press "NPR" setting for natural pressure release. It takes 8-10 times for all inside pressure to release.
- Cook for more time in the mix is too watery.
- Open the pot and arrange the cooked recipe in serving plates. Enjoy the vegan recipe!

Nutrition:

- Calories - 246
- Fat - 4g
- Carbs - 21g
- Protein - 11.5g

COCONUT MEATBALLS

Preparation time: 10 minutes

Cooking time: 4 hours

Serving: 4

Ingredients:

- 1 and ½ pounds beef
- 2 small yellow onions, chopped
- 1 egg
- A pinch of sea salt
- Black pepper to the taste
- 3 tablespoons cilantro, chopped
- 14 ounces canned coconut milk
- 2 tablespoons hot sauce
- 1 teaspoon basil, dried
- 1 tablespoon green curry paste
- 1 tablespoon coconut aminos

Directions:

- Put the meat in a bowl, add 1 small onion, egg, salt, pepper and 1 tablespoon cilantro, stir well, shape medium-sized meatballs and place them in your slow cooker.
- Add hot sauce, aminos, coconut milk, curry paste and basil, toss to cover all meatballs and cook on Low for 4 hours.
- Arrange meatballs on a platter and serve with the sauce drizzled all over.
- Enjoy!

Nutrition:

- Calories - 200
- Fat - 6
- Carbs - 8
- Protein - 4

PEANUT CHICKEN STRIPS

Preparation time: 15 minutes

Cooking time: 6 hours

Serving: 7

Ingredients:

- 3 tablespoons peanut butter, melted
- 1-pound chicken breast, boneless, skinless
- 1 teaspoon paprika
- 1 teaspoon salt
- 1 teaspoon olive oil
- 2 tablespoons almond flour
- 1 teaspoon cayenne pepper

Directions:

- Cut the chicken breast into the thick strips.
- Then sprinkle the chicken strips with the paprika, salt, and cayenne pepper.
- Coat the chicken strips in the almond flour. Pour the olive oil into the slow cooker and add the coated chicken strips.
- Close the slow cooker lid and cook the chicken strips for 4 hours on HIGH. Open the slow cooker lid and stir the chicken strips carefully.
- Close the lid and cook the snack for 2 hours more on LOW. Chill the chicken strips very well. Serve!

Nutrition:

- Calories - 161
- Fat - 9.5
- Carbs - 3.15
- Protein - 16

ZUCCHINI AND EGGPLANT PATE

Preparation time: 5 minutes

Cooking time: 3 hours

Serving: 4

Ingredients:

- 2 tablespoons lemon juice
- ¼ cup vegetable stock
- 1 eggplant, cubed
- 2 zucchinis, cubed
- 2 tablespoons olive oil
- 3 garlic cloves
- A pinch of salt and black pepper

Directions:

- In your slow cooker, combine all the ingredients, cover and cook on low for 3 hours.
- Blend with an immersion blender, divide into bowls and serve as a party spread.

Nutrition:

- Calories - 110
- Fat - 7,6
- Carbs - 11
- Protein - 2,5

CHEESY TACO DIP

Serving: 2

Preparation time: 10 minutes

Cooking time: 1 hour

Ingredients:

- 1/2 lb ground beef, browned
- 1/2 oz taco seasoning mix
- 8 oz tomatoes, crushed
- 1/2 lb cheese, shredded

Directions:

- Combine all ingredients in the crockpot. Add 1/4 cup water. Mix thoroughly.
- Cover and cook on high for 1 hour.

Nutrition:

- Calories - 163
- Fat - 11.6 g
- Carbs - 5.1 g
- Protein - 9.8 g

PARTY CHILI TURKEY

Preparation time: 5 minutes

Cooking time: 4 hours

Serving: 4

Ingredients:

- 1 pound ground smoked turkey
- 12 ounces chili sauce

Directions:

- In your slow cooker, combine all the ingredients, cover and cook on low for 4 hours.
- Arrange on a platter and serve as an appetizer.

Nutrition:

- Calories - 122
- Fat - 1,5
- Carbs - 6
- Protein - 20,7

CANDIED PECANS

Preparation + Cooking time: 30 minutes

Serving: 30

Ingredients:

- 1 tsp butter
- 4 cups raw pecans
- ¼ cup Erythritol
- 1 tsp ground cinnamon
- ½ tsp ground nutmeg
- 1/8 tsp ground ginger
- 1/8 tsp cayenne pepper
- Pinch of sea salt
- ½ cup filtered water

Directions:

- Place the butter in the Instant Pot and select "Saute". Then, add all ingredients except water and cook for about 5 minutes, stirring frequently.
- Select the "Cancel" and stir in water.
- Secure the lid and place the pressure valve to "Seal" position.
- Select "MANUAL" and cook under "High Pressure" for about 10 minutes.
- Meanwhile, preheat the oven to 350 degrees F.
- Select the "Cancel" and carefully do a "Natural" release for about 10 minutes and then do a "Quick" release.
- Remove the lid and Bake for about 5 minutes.
- Remove from oven and keep aside to cool before serving.

Nutrition:

- Calories - 28
- Fat - 2.7g
- Carbs - 0.08g
- Protein - 0.3g

DESSERTS

CHOCOLATE THINS

Preparation time: 20 minutes

Cooking time: 40 minutes

Serving: 5

Ingredients:

- 2 tablespoons almonds, chopped
- 2 oz dark chocolate
- 1 tablespoon coconut oil

Directions:

- Put dark chocolate and coconut oil in the crockpot.
- Close the lid and cook the ingredients for 40 minutes on High.
- Meanwhile, line the baking tray with the baking paper.
- When the time is finished, the chocolate mixture should be homogenous.
- With the help of the spoon, pour the chocolate mixture in the baking paper. You should get small rounds (1 tablespoon = 1 chocolate round.
- Then sprinkle every chocolate round with almonds.
- Chill the thins until firm (about 1 hour in the fridge).
- Remove the cooked chocolate thins from the baking paper and store them in the glass jar.

Nutrition:

- Calories - 101
- Fat - 7.9
- Carbs - 6.9
- Protein - 0.9

CREAMY VANILLA CAKE

Preparation + Cooking time: 35 minutes

Serving: 8

Ingredients:

- For the crust: 5 eggs
- 2 ½ cups almond flour
- ¼ cup swerve
- 1 tbsp baking powder
- 3 tbsp coconut oil
- 4 tbsp cocoa powder, unsweetened
- ¼ cup milk

- For the cream cheese layer: 2 cups mascarpone cheese
- ¼ cup whipped cream, unsweetened
- 2 tsp vanilla extract
- ¼ cup swerve

Directions:

- Plug in the instant pot and position a trivet in the inner pot. Pour in one cup of water and set aside.
- In a large mixing bowl, combine together almond flour, swerve, baking powder, and cocoa powder. Mix well and then add eggs, coconut oil, and milk. Using a hand mixer beat well on high speed. Pour the mixture into the lightly greased springform pan and wrap with some aluminum foil.
- Place the pan on the trivet and seal the lid. Set the steam release handle to the "Sealing" position and press the "MANUAL" button.
- Set the timer for 15 minutes on high pressure.
- When done, perform a quick pressure release and open the lid. Remove the pan from the pot and chill for a while.
- Meanwhile, combine together mascarpone, whipped cream, vanilla extract, and swerve. Beat well with a hand mixer. Optionally, add some more sweetener or vanilla extract.
- Pour the cream mixture over the chilled crust and flatten the surface with a kitchen spatula.
- Refrigerate for at least two hours before serving.

Nutrition:

- Calories - 266
- Fat - 21.7g
- Carbs - 5g
- Protein - 13.1g

TOMATO PIE

Preparation time: 10 minutes

Cooking time: 3 hours

Serving: 6

Ingredients:

- 1 and ½ cups whole wheat flour
- 1 teaspoon cinnamon powder
- 1 teaspoon baking soda
- 1 teaspoon baking powder
- ¾ cup coconut sugar
- 1 cup tomatoes, blanched, peeled and chopped
- ½ cup olive oil
- 2 tablespoons apple cider vinegar
- Cooking spray

Directions:

- In a bowl, mix flour with sugar, cinnamon, baking powder and soda and stir well.
- In another bowl, mix tomatoes with oil and cider vinegar and stir very well.
- Combine the 2 mixtures, stir, pour everything into your slow cooker greased with cooking spray, cover and cook on High for 3 hours.
- Leave the pie aside to cool down, slice and serve.
- Enjoy!

Nutrition:

- Calories - 220
- Fat - 8
- Carbs - 11
- Protein - 3

TIRAMISU BREAD PUDDING

Serving: 6

Ingredients:

- Bread Pudding
- ½ cup water
- ½ cup granulated sugar
- 1 tablespoon espresso powder
- 2 tablespoons Kahlua
- 1½ cups whole milk
- ½ cup heavy cream
- 5 large eggs
- 8 cups cubed (1-inch pieces French bread
- Topping
- ½ cup heavy cream
- ½ cup mascarpone cheese
- 1 tablespoon granulated sugar
- 1 teaspoon vanilla extract
- Unsweetened cocoa, for dusting

Directions:

- Spray the slow cooker with nonstick cooking spray.
- In a saucepan, mix together the water, sugar and espresso powder. Bring to boil and stir until the espresso has completely dissolved. Remove from the heat, stir in the Kahlua, and set aside.
- In a mixing bowl, combine the eggs, milk, and cream, stirring until the eggs are completely incorporated. Pour in the cooled Kahlua mixture.
- Take the cubed French bread and stir it into the milk mixture, pushing the bread down and stirring until all the bread cubes have been covered.
- Make the topping by beating together the cream, mascarpone, sugar, and vanilla. Mix until fluffy and thick.
- Serve a scoop of bread pudding with a dollop of topping. Enjoy!

Nutrition:

- Calories - 291
- Fat - 19.4 g
- Carbs - 24.3 g
- Protein - 4.6 g

QUICK CHOCOLATE CAKE

Preparation + Cooking time: 17 minutes

Serving: 12

Ingredients:

- 1 cup applesauce, unsweetened
- 3 large eggs
- 1 cup dark chocolate chips, unsweetened
- 1 tsp vanilla extract, sugar-free
- ¼ cup raw cocoa powder, unsweetened
- ½ cup arrowroot powder
- 3 tsp coconut oil, melted
- ½ tsp salt

Directions:

- Plug in your instant pot and pour 2 cups of water in the stainless steel insert. Position a trivet and place the ramekin filled with chocolate chips on top. Press "Sautee" button bring the water to a boil. Cook until melted and remove the ramekin from the pot.
- In a large mixing bowl, combine eggs, vanilla extract, and applesauce. Mix until combined. Now, add cocoa powder, arrowroot powder, salt, and melted chocolate chips.
- Brush 6-inches springform pan with melted coconut oil and pour in the previously prepared mixture. Place on top of a trivet and securely lock the lid.
- Adjust the steam release handle and press the "MANUAL" button. Set the timer for 5 minutes.
- Cook on high pressure.
- When done, perform a quick release of the pressure by turning the handle to a venting position.
- Open the pot and let it chill for 10 minutes.

Nutrition:

- Calories - 107
- Fat - 5.3g
- Carbs - 13.3g
- Protein - 2.6g

WALNUT PUMPKIN MUG CAKE

Preparation + Cooking time: 50 minutes

Serving: 2

Ingredients:

- ½ cup almond flour
- 1 tbsp almonds, roughly chopped
- 1 tbsp walnuts, roughly chopped
- 1 tbsp chia seeds
- 1 tbsp pumpkin seeds
- 1 tbsp coconut oil, melted
- 1 tsp baking powder

Spices:

- ¼ tsp salt
- 2 tsp stevia powder
- ¼ tsp apple pie spice mix

Directions:

- Combine almond flour, almonds, walnuts, chia seeds, pumpkin seeds, and baking powder in a large mixing bowl. Add melted coconut oil, stevia powder, and apple pie spice mix.
- Mix until well incorporated.
- Pour the mixture into oven safe mugs and optionally, top with some dark chocolate chips.
- Plug in the instant pot and pour 1 cup of water in the stainless steel insert. Place the trivet on the bottom and set the mugs on the top. Securely lock the lid and adjust the steam release handle. Press the "MANUAL" button and se the timer for 2 minutes on "High" pressure.
- When you hear the cooker's end signal, perform a quick pressure release and open the pot. Carefully remove mugs from the pot and let it chill for 10 minutes before serving.
- Optionally, top with some extra pumpkin seeds.

Nutrition:

- Calories - 363
- Fat - 30.2g
- Carbs - 6.2g
- Protein - 11g

KETO CHERRY MOUSSE

Preparation + Cooking time: 15 minutes

Serving: 6

Ingredients:

- 1 ½ cup whipping cream
- 1/2 cup whole milk

- 1/4 cup erythritol
- 5 large egg yolks; beaten
- 1/2 cup coconut cream
- 1 tablespoon pecans; minced
- 2 teaspoon cherry extract
- 1/2 teaspoon salt

Directions:

- Combine whipping cream, egg yolks, erytthritol, milk, salt, and coconut cream in a medium-sized saucepan over a medium-high heat. Stir well and heat up without
- boiling. Remove from the heat and pour the mixture into oven-safe ramekins. Sprinkle with minced pecans and wrap each ramekin with aluminum foil, Set aside
- Plug in your instant pot and pour 1 cup of water in the stainless steel insert. Set the trivet on the bottom and place the ramekins on top
- Securely lock the lid and adjust the steam release handle by moving the valve to the "SEALING" position. Set the timer for 7 minutes on "MANUAL" mode
- When you hear the cooker's end signal, perform a quick pressure release and open the pot. Refrigerate for at least an hour before serving.

Nutrition:

- Calories - 223
- Fat - 21.8g
- Carbs - 13.2g
- Protein - 4.5g

HOT FUDGE CAKE

Serving: 12

Ingredients:

- 2 cups maple syrup
- 2 flax eggs
- 2 cups flour
- ¾ cup cocoa powder
- 1 cup vegan milk
- ½ cup vegan butter (or coconut oil
- 1 tablespoon baking powder
- 2 teaspoons vanilla extract
- 1 cup water (as needed)

Directions:

- Combine all ingredients in a large bowl, whisking together and adding water as needed.
- Grease the inside of the slow cooker and pour in the batter.
- Cook covered on low for 3 hours until cake has set. Use a toothpick to determine when it is ready.

Nutrition:

- Calories - 349
- Fat - 13 g
- Carbs - 57 g
- Protein - 4 g

LAVA CAKE

Preparation time: 10 minutes

Cooking time: 3.5 hours

Serving: 4

Ingredients:

- 1/3 cup Swerve
- ¼ cup almond flour
- 1 ½ tablespoon cocoa powder
- ¾ teaspoon salt
- ¼ teaspoon baking powder
- ½ teaspoon lemon juice
- 3 tablespoons butter
- 2 eggs, beaten
- ¼ cup of water
- 1 teaspoon vanilla extract
- Cooking spray

Directions:

- Mix up together almond flour, Swerve, cocoa powder, salt, baking powder, butter, and eggs.
- Then add water, lemon juice, and vanilla extract.
- Mix up the lava cake mixture with the help of the hand mixer.
- Spray the crockpot bottom with the cooking spray.
- Pour the lava cake mixture in the crockpot and flatten it with the help of the spatula.
- Close the lid and cook the dessert for 3.5 hours on Low.
- Chill the lava cake well before serving.

Nutrition:

- Calories - 126
- Fat - 12
- Carbs - 2.1
- Protein - 3.6

SHORTBREAD COOKIES

Preparation time: 15 minutes

Cooking time: 1 hour

Serving: 3

Ingredients:

- ½ cup almond flour
- ½ teaspoon vanilla extract
- 1 tablespoon Erythritol
- 1 tablespoon butter
- ½ teaspoon avocado oil

Directions:

- In the mixing bowl, mix up together Erythritol and almond flour.
- Then add vanilla extract and butter.
- Knead the soft but non-sticky dough.
- Brush the crockpot bowl with avocado oil from inside.
- Make the small balls from the dough and press them gently with the help of the fork.
- Put the cookies in the crockpot and cook for 1 hour on High.

Nutrition:

- Calories - 64
- Fat - 6.3
- Carbs - 6.1
- Protein - 1.1

STRAWBERRY PANCAKES

Preparation + Cooking time: 45 minutes

Serving: 3

Ingredients:

- 1 cup cream cheese
- 1/2 tablespoon psyllium husk powder
- 5 large eggs
- 1 teaspoon vanilla extract
- 1/4 cup coconut flour
- 2 tablespoon butter
- 1/4 teaspoon salt
- For the topping: 1/2 teaspoon stevia powder
- 1/2 strawberry extract
- 1 cup whipped cream

Directions:

- In a large mixing bowl, combine coconut flour, psyllium husk powder, and salt. Mix well and then gradually add eggs. Beat with an electric mixer for 3 minutes.
- Now; add butter, cream cheese, and vanilla extract. Continue to beat until all well combined, Set aside

- Plug in the instant pot and grease the stainless steel insert with some cooking spray. Pour about 1/3 of the mixture in the pot and close the lid. Adjust the steam release handle and press the "MANUAL" button. Set the timer for 3 minutes. Cook on "HIGH" pressure.
- When done, perform a quick pressure release and carefully Now; prepare the topping. Combine all ingredients in a large bowl and mix until well combined. Divide the mixture evenly and top each pancake.

Nutrition:

- Calories - 618
- Fat - 156.3g
- Carbs - 6.7g
- Protein - 18.6g

ORANGE PUDDING

Preparation time: 10 minutes

Cooking time: 5 hours and 3 minutes

Serving: 4

Ingredients:

- Cooking spray
- 1 teaspoon baking powder
- 1 cup almond flour
- 1 cup palm sugar
- ½ teaspoon cinnamon, ground
- 3 tablespoons coconut oil, melted
- ½ cup almond milk
- ½ cup pecans, chopped
- ¾ cup water
- ½ cup raisins
- ½ cup orange peel, grated
- ¾ cup orange juice
- Chopped pecans for serving

Directions:

- Spray your slow cooker with cooking spray.
- In a bowl, mix flour with half of the sugar, baking powder and cinnamon and stir.
- Add 2 tablespoons oil and milk and stir again well.
- Add pecans and raisins, stir and pour this into slow cooker.
- Heat up a small pan over medium high heat, add water, orange juice, orange peel, the rest of the oil and the remaining sugar, stir, bring to a boil, pour over the mix in the slow cooker, cover and cook on Low for 5 hours.
- Divide into dessert bowls and serve with chopped pecans on top.
- Enjoy!

Nutrition:

- Calories - 222
- Fat - 3
- Carbs - 8
- Protein - 6

CHOCOLATE CUPCAKES

Preparation + Cooking time: 20 minutes

Serving: 6

Ingredients:

- 1 ½ cups of almond flour
- 1/4 cup cream cheese
- 1/4 cup swerve
- 2 tablespoon cocoa powder; unsweetened.
- 1 cup shredded coconut
- 2 large eggs
- 3 tablespoon butter
- 2 teaspoon baking powder
- 1/4 cup blueberries
- 3 tablespoon plain Greek yogurt
- 1 teaspoon vanilla extract

Directions:

- In a large mixing bowl, combine together eggs and butter. Beat well on high speed until light and fluffy mixture. Then add swerve, cream cheese, and Greek yogurt.
- Continue to mix until smooth.
- Finally, add almond flour, shredded coconut, and baking powder. Mix well again and fold in blueberries.
- Divide the mixture between 6 silicone cups and set aside
- Plug in the instant pot and position a trivet at the bottom of the inner pot. Pour in 1 cup of water and carefully place cups on the trivet
- Seal the lid and set the steam release handle to the "SEALING" position. Set the timer for 10 minutes on the "MANUAL" mode
- Perform a quick pressure release and open the lid. Remove the cups from the pot and cool to a room temperature

Nutrition:

- Calories - 212
- Fat - 18.9g
- Carbs - 4.2g
- Protein - 6g

COCOA VANILLA PUDDING

Preparation + Cooking time: 10 minutes

Serving: 3

Ingredients:

- 1 cup cream cheese
- ¼ cup coconut oil
- 5 large eggs whites
- 5 large egg yolks
- 1 tsp erythritol
- 3 tsp raw cocoa powder
- ½ tsp glucomannan powder
- Spices: 1 tsp vanilla extract
- ½ tsp lemon zest, freshly grated
- ¼ tsp nutmeg, ground

Directions:

- Plug in the instant pot and place cream cheese in the stainless steel insert. Press the "Saute" button gently stir with a wooden spatula.
- Stir in the egg yolks, cocoa, erythritol, coconut oil, and glucomannan powder. Cook for 2-3 minutes, or until all well incorporated. Turn off the pot.
- In a large bowl, combine egg whites, vanilla extract, and ground nutmeg.
- With a hand mixer, beat until foamy.
- Spoon the egg whites into the pot and give it a good stir.
- Pour the mixture into a serving bowl while still hot. Set aside to cool completely.
- Refrigerate for 1 hour and optionally, sprinkle with some raw cocoa before serving.
- Enjoy!
- Calories - 554
- Fat - 53.1g
- Carbs - 4.2g
- Protein - 16.7g

CHERRY CLAFOUTIS

Serving: 6

Ingredients:

- 1 pound fresh cherries (or use a jar of cherries in natural juice or brandy, drained but with the juices retained
- ¼ cup butter
- 4 large eggs
- 2 extra egg yolks
- ¾ cup white sugar
- ½ cup all-purpose flour, sifted
- 1..." cups whole milk

Directions:

- Remove the pot from your slow cooker and heat the base on high while you are preparing the ingredients.

- Use 1 tablespoon of the butter to butter the sides of the pot, then melt the rest of the butter in the microwave and set aside to cool down.
- In a mixing bowl, mix together the eggs, yolks, and sugar. Mix or whisk in the melted butter, flour, and the milk to form a light batter.
- Pour the cherries into the buttered pot, then pour the batter over the top.
- Cook on high for 3-4 hours or until the clafoutis is set.

Nutrition:

- Calories - 252
- Fat - 9.8 g
- Carbs - 34.2 g
- Protein - 6.8 g

CROCK POT CHEESECAKE

Serving: 6-8

Ingredients:

- 2-3 cups water
- 6 whole graham crackers crushed into crumbs
- 3 tablespoons butter, melted
- 24
- ounces
- cream cheese,
- ¾ cup sugar
- 3 large eggs

Directions:

- Fill the slow cooker with water. Water level must be lower than cake pan for cheesecake but enough not to dry up while cooking, about 2-3 cups depending on the size of the cooker.
- In a bowl, mix crumbs and butter together. Blend well.
- Press the crumbs down evenly on bottom of pan to form the cake's crust.
- In another bowl, combine cream cheese and sugar. Mix until well-blended. Add eggs one at a time, blending well after adding each one.
- Pour cream cheese mixture over the graham cracker crust and spread evenly.
- Place in the slow cooker and cover.
- Cook for 2 hours to 2 hours and 30 minutes on HIGH. Cheesecake is done when center in no longer soft and sides begin to crack.
- Allow to cool down for about an hour.
- Remove from cooker and allow to set in the refrigerator for at least an hour before serving.

Nutrition:

- Calories - 257
- Fat - 18 g
- Carbs - 20.4 g

- Protein - 4.4 g

ALMOND VANILLA BROWNIES

Preparation + Cooking time: 35 minutes

Serving: 6

Ingredients:

- 3/4 cup almond flour
- 1/4 cup raw almonds; finely chopped
- 1/4 cup cocoa powder; unsweetened.
- 1/3 cup coconut cream
- 4 tablespoon granulated stevia
- 2 teaspoon baking powder
- 1/4 cup flaxseed meal
- 3 large eggs
- 2 tablespoon butter; melted
- 2 teaspoon vanilla extract

Directions:

- In a medium-sized bowl, combine together almond flour, flaxseed meal, cocoa powder, stevia, and baking powder. Mix well and then add eggs, butter, vanilla extract, chopped almonds, and coconut cream. Using a hand mixer beat well until fully incorporated.
- Line a fitting cake pan with some parchment paper. Pour in the batter and shake the pan a couple of times to flatten the surface. Tightly wrap with aluminum foil and set aside.
- Now plug in the instant pot and position a trivet at the bottom of the inner pot. Pour in two cups of water and carefully place the pan on the trivet
- Seal the lid and set the steam release handle. Press the "MANUAL" button and cook for 25 minutes on high pressure.
- When done, perform a quick pressure release and open the lid. Remove the pan and cool completely before slicing

Nutrition:

- Calories - 158
- Fat - 13.5g
- Carbs - 2.7g
- Protein - 5.9g

FRUITCAKE

Serving: 16

Ingredients:

- 1 1/2 cups flour
- 2/3 cup pineapple juice
- Coat the inside of the slow cooker with nonstick cooking spray.

- In a bowl, combine the flour, baking powder, sucanat, and cinnamon.
- Stir in the chopped apples to coat in the mixture.
- Combine the mashed banana and vanilla, then mix it in with the flour mixture. Add just enough water to moisten the batter, if needed.
- Divide the cake into equal to control the calories per serving. Best served warm.
- 1/8 tsp baking soda
- 1 cup unsweetened crushed pineapple, drained
- 1 1/2 tsp baking powder
- 1/2 cup softened unsalted butter
- 4 eggs, separated
- 1 cup sucanat
- 1 1/2 cups golden raisins
- 4 oz candied cherries, halved
- 4 oz mixed candied fruit
- 1 cup slivered almonds
- 1/2 tsp almond extract
- 1/2 tsp vanilla extract
- Non-stick cooking spray

Directions:

- Coat a cake pan with nonstick cooking spray.
- Beat the butter and sucanat until creamy using an electric mixer. Add the yolks and mix well.
- In a bowl, combine the baking powder and flour, then add gradually into the yolk mixture, alternating between it and the pineapple juice.
- Fold the raisins, crushed pineapple, candied fruit, and extract into the batter.
- In a separate bowl, whip the egg whites until stiff, then fold into the batter.
- Pour the mixture into the prepared cake pan and cover with aluminum foil. Place the pan on a rack in the slow cooker and pour about half a cup of warm water around the pan.
- Cover and cook for 4 hours on high. Set aside to rest for 10 minutes before removing the cake.
- Set aside to cool before slicing. Slice evenly into 16 servings to control calories per serving.

Nutrition:

- Calories - 276.75

Printed in Great Britain
by Amazon